# Understanding Fear

*The key to a brighter future*

Dick Stoute

B.Eng, M.B.A. M.Phil

Revive Publications

Copyright © 2011 by Dick Stoute

All rights reserved. This book, or parts thereof, may not be reproduced in any form without permission.

*A catalogue record for this book is available from the British Library*

Cover illustration by Suzette Chin-Humphrey

Cover design by Jehanne Silva-Freimane

ISBN: 978-1-907962-24-0

Published by Revive Publications

Reading, England

http://understandingfear-das.blogspot.com

# Contents

| | | |
|---|---|---|
| Introduction | | 7 |
| 1 | Our War Paradigm | 13 |
| 2 | Social Responses to Fear | 34 |
| 3 | The Hierarchy of Fear | 66 |
| 4 | Fearful Myths | 86 |
| 5 | Summary<br>Where we are coming from<br>Where we are now<br>Where we are going | 120 |
| 6 | Psycho Fractals | 126 |
| 7 | Goals | 146 |
| 8 | War Paradigm to Learning Paradigm | 163 |
| 9 | The Learning Paradigm | 189 |
| 10 | Strategy for the Learning Paradigm | 200 |
| Bibliography | | 233 |

# Introduction

As the fire of revolution spreads through the Arab world we, once again, are invited to consider the question: Are we heading for doom and destruction, or are we on a path to paradise? How can we find an answer to this question?

It is usual to track where politics or technology is going and use this to build a futuristic world. I have taken a different path. I seek to predict the future by first getting a better understanding of human nature. This has produced an amazing result, which I present to you here.

There are many apparent deficiencies in our present society. These are mainly attached to what we consider to be failures in human behavior. They include crime, greed, aggression and all forms of mental and physical violence. Although technology may play a role, it does not drive these tendencies to antisocial behavior and we need to look to something other than technology to solve the problem.

Our religions speak to this problem, but with a gradually weakening voice, and it is very unlikely that these ancient philosophies can be beneficially applied to the new millennium. A new approach is needed.

As educational levels rise we become more curious and less likely to accept ancient truths without critical examination. Traditional spiritual beliefs are being questioned and new ideas are emerging. Educated people are leaving the congregation of the faithful. Despite the worst fears of these communities, those that choose rationality over the old ideas seem quite capable of maintaining good humanistic behavior, while religion is still an ongoing cause of warfare.

There is growing uncertainty brought on by rapid social change. This is driven by technology and the accumulation of knowledge. The traditional fear of God's wrath is being replaced by the fear of social and environmental disaster. Technology has not resulted in reduced fear of the future; instead it seems to heighten it as we instantly learn of foreign wars and disasters. Our propensity to fear is not diminished.

Social systems, such as those that dispense justice, are being recognized as inefficient and as inappropriate for the future, but we are not sure what will replace them and little effort is made to improve them. Despite the need to focus attention in this area, we focus our intellectual resources on increased efficiency in the production of goods which are already in oversupply.

The economic mechanisms of society continue to concentrate resources into the hands of the rich while making the poor relatively poorer. The capitalist dream is undermined by this uneven income distribution. As poor participants are sidelined due to a lack of purchasing power markets tend to shrink. This can temporarily be overcome by encouraging the poor to borrow and consume, but as we have recently seen, this leads to instability.

*Understanding Fear*

There are many doom predictors. The growing inequality of incomes feeds a fear that the whole economic system will collapse. There is a rising fear of economic slavery, while environmental concerns get more urgent daily. Few commentators express hope for a better future; most anticipate a more difficult existence. We seem to have to work harder to maintain our positions while the air is full of threats to our way of life. There is a confusing abundance of choice available for any product. The quality of the merchandise is good, the level of service is excellent, but we are not happy.

Despite these negative trends, and legitimate concerns, the future is very bright. The long struggle for existence is coming to an end. Existence is no longer our prime concern, we have achieved success. We now have to shift our perspective and focus on understanding our fear response and how this shapes our society; this will enable us to enjoy the benefits of our technology and to move beyond the war paradigm.

*Introduction*

This book is about how our society is evolving to a brighter future. It brings together information from several diverse sources and draws attention to the relationships between them – the consistent patterns of behavior from a wide range of human experiences. It is unusual in that it seeks to establish a model of human behavior and then applies it to develop a path to the future. To follow these arguments, you need to see our society with new eyes and understand how we became embroiled in a war paradigm in the first place and how we adapted to this environment. I hope you enjoy the book and that you learn something by reading it.

# Chapter 1

# Our War Paradigm

We all yearn for life without war and much effort is directed at achieving this happy state of existence; but in the midst of our striving to end war we have a religion and a society geared to propagate it. There is a war psychology surrounding us that not only helps us to fight but also helps to get wars started. As we go about our daily lives we are immersed in this war paradigm and automatically react in a way that propagates it. To get a glimpse of it let me take you to a distant location far away from daily life, a position from which you can get an overview of society and can see the effects of the war paradigm. To do this we have to ignore details and just look at prominent trends.

Our distant ancestors lived without war, while developing the technology for producing more and more food. There may not have been war but there was undoubtedly intra-tribe violence and inter-tribal territory clashes. Our ancestors successfully developed food-producing technologies and this removed the restraints that kept their population in check. War followed – rather than inter-tribal territory clashes there were now all out wars to destroy opposing tribes. **Let me emphasize this. At some point in our history we became our own worst enemy.** We then evolved a society, a religion and a culture to live in these circumstances. Our current belief systems and organizational structures were developed in response to this environment, one that dictated that we had to fight each other to survive.

When the ancients first encountered war they had to develop a technology to fight. It was immediately obvious that there was strength in numbers and a means of organizing large bands of people to fight for a common cause was essential. To achieve this fear had to be used to control and motivate.

This created the need for new religions. The fertility cults that held sway when fertility was the most important ingredient of survival gave way to religions that supported the new threat; other people. If you compare say Old Testament doctrines with what a society has to do to organize itself for war you can find several similarities. A central authority is needed along with a means of stimulating the population to fight (kill the unbeliever). Spiritual beliefs were used to facilitate this process by replicating the social situation. This resulted in war gods being created in the image of war chiefs; tough gods that instituted tough love practices. These gods faced the same problems as their earthly counterparts and over the passage of time, best practices were incorporated into the religious lore as instructions from God.

The Biblical stories emphasized the need to follow the directions of the leaders and illustrated that a terrible fate awaited any dissenters. The story of the Garden of Eden in Genesis illustrates the trauma of the transition from a fertility cult, controlled by women, to a war religion where men dominated. The power of the fertility symbol "woman" had to be discredited and blamed for the problems being faced

– the need to fight. The concept of "good and evil" emerged and became the main conceptual building block for the religions that followed.

I emphasize that these things were not done out of any evil intent. Survival was at stake and these techniques were largely responsible for their race being successful in its bid to survive as a separate entity. Victory in war was essential and farmers and herders had to be converted into warriors to achieve this. It was a very successful technique and was continually repeated by many tribes; it also became an unquestioned foundation to the societies that developed.

To put it another way, the fear of going to war had to be overcome by an even greater fear, that of offending their God. Desperate times invoked desperate means, and we can appreciate that these measures are necessary when faced with hostilities. But this technique became so ingrained in our society that we can't perceive it as a socially propagated psychology, which dominates every aspect of our social activity. Without changing the basic tenants, we have simply migrated away from

*Our War Paradigm*

fighting with weapons to fighting with words and laws.

War is a state of mind. We have developed many forms of warfare, and have structured all of our social institutions so that they will be effective at fighting wars. We are a war-based society and everything we do is interpreted in the context of a war. Our local newspapers are excellent at converting every issue into a most sensational battle report. From the sports pages "Zimbabwe route Pakistan" through politics, religion, law and business.

I invite you to record the number of battles reported in the daily newspapers. Include the business battles, letters to the editor with personal vendettas, or supporting a particular campaign. Don't forget the political battles, fought with claims of victory designed to convince the troops that the battles are being won. Also include the advertising battles; where competitors fight it out for market share, reports on the proceedings of the courts, and the medical reports where the fight against disease is recorded.

## Understanding Fear

It is a well known fact that more newspapers are sold when sensational battle reports are included. Editors compete with each other to see who can come up with the most aggressive headlines and wherever reports can be made to generate conflict this is done. We expect this behavior. This is because we accept that newspapers, like everyone else, have to go to war with their competitors to survive.

Every organization in our society is conceptualized as fighting wars. When not actually engaged in battle, we are preparing for it. Companies battle their competition. Politicians continue their war of words, not only at election time, but throughout their career. Our religious leaders preach sermons of hell and brimstone in their fight against the evil influence of the devil. The police are constantly fighting crime. There is a fight against drugs, poverty, disease and anything else you may care to imagine.

Our television is used primarily to highlight conflict, be it news, soap opera, movie, or documentary. This theme is continued in our comic strips and cartoons where the good guys or super heroes fight the bad guys. No one challenges the evil intent of the bad guys. It is accepted without question that they wish to conquer the earth and make everyone slaves.

Our organizations are structured in the best way possible to fight a war. There is a definite chain of command. Each person's responsibility is well defined. The person at the top is given Godlike status over the whole organization, while at each intermediate level the person in charge adopts this same superior stance in relation to those lower in the hierarchy. No one can question their boss as he has superior information and a direct line to those above. The boss decides what information to pass up the ladder and what to pass down. This gives him almost unlimited power over those under him in the hierarchy. Everyone must take orders from those above them in the chain, if they don't they are banished from the tribe.

This theme of spiritual war and man's position in the eternal conflict has evolved in its transition from the Jewish Old Testament to the Christian New Testament. In the Old Testament, God dishes out his own punishment and Satan appears as a messenger of God, while in the New Testament Satan evolved to become the leader of a rebel band of fallen angels. In the early Christian church, Satan is seen as propagating evil; he infiltrates the ranks of the faithful and turns them away from the true path. This evolution allows the Christian God to be cast as pure good and Satan as pure evil, an evolution from the God of the Old Testament who is cast as a tough tribal king with Satan as his servant.

The leaders of the early Christian church perfected the technique of seeing the devil's work in anything that appeared to oppose them. They swiftly accused anyone who came up against them of being under the control of Satan. This technique worked well and facilitated the elimination of dissenting views from the ranks of the faithful.

This approach to opposition was not limited to the church. Over the years it expanded and found applications throughout society. It is used to eliminate anyone who does not conform to the norm, or who threatens the power structure. This theme of good fighting bad reoccurs constantly.

*Our War Paradigm*

Each individual or group who feels threatened uses this same approach to deal with the threat. This leads to continual warfare, as once judged as evil, and under the devil's influence, there is no recourse. You can't negotiate with pure evil, as the devil will manipulate you. Those contaminated by evil have to be eliminated, removed from the face of the Earth. This justifies genocide. There is no path to peace, no means of negotiation. The Inquisition is a good example of this approach. Good fights evil and the cycle continues, but it only happens when there is a high level of fear. When fear dissipates a different gentler pattern emerges.

While we live in a society designed and looking for wars, we spend most of our lives trying to cooperate as best we can with those around us. If you walk down a crowded sidewalk, you will notice that people are cooperating to ensure that the traffic flows smoothly. Where space conflicts arise among pedestrians these are efficiently dealt with. Similarly, on a highway in our smaller communities, cooperation is more evident than conflict. In a well-run business, employees are doing their best to achieve well-defined and agreed goals. The so-called competition of the private sector masks a hive of activity all directed at cooperating fully with the whole supply chain. This theme is picked up in "No Contest" by Alfie Kohn who argues that competition is counter-productive and "The death of competition" by James F. Moore who illustrates that the business world is very similar to an ecosystem.

In this context, winning is not achieved through giving orders and instilling fear in employees, instead it is achieved through cooperating to provide a service for customers. Even the top management is involved in this process and facilitates it through the correct application of resources and liaising with the various teams to achieve the stated goals. One of the tenants of TQM (Total Quality Management is one of the techniques used in businesses) is "eliminate fear from the workplace". By a simple extension of logic, this goal, when applied to society as a whole, leads to the knowledge paradigm. This is where business is heading, but along the way it will have to drop the psychology of the master-slave relationships it has inherited from its warring ancestors.

*Our War Paradigm*

Slavery was a natural result of war. Instead of killing the enemy you could get them to work for you. The concept was built into the emerging War God religions between 4,000 and 1,000 BC. The Bible discusses slavery as if it is a natural feature of the social landscape. (James Michener in his book "The Covenant" makes the point that the Dutch used the Bible to justify their taking of slaves during their conquest of South Africa.)

The best way of controlling slaves was to have them adopt your religion as this either removed their group identity, or stigmatized them as inferior. The fact that they lost the battle demonstrated that your God was stronger than theirs and in their state of shock and disillusion they were quite easily influenced to switch. In later years, when slavery became institutionalized for its economic benefits, it was left to the well organized Church to follow up the victory with the teachings which would remove whatever self confidence remained in the conquered tribe and replace it with a self perpetuating fear of the Christian God. In hostile times it is essential to ensure that your slaves, and indeed your entire population, were content to work very hard with little or no reward, so that the society could accumulate the resources needed to continue fighting without having to worry about revolt. This combination of war and religion helped the British to create an empire.

The concepts, in the Christian religion, which achieved this control over conquered people have been transferred to the economic environment so seamlessly that the "Capitalist system" has survived a long and fruitful reign, living on the same techniques. These are part of the "mental chains" that enslave us. We can see this in the concepts that are applied to corporations.

A company is a slave to its owners and it is still generally accepted that it is the duty of the employees to maximize the wealth of the shareholders, just as it was the duty of a slave to work for the enrichment of his master. In law, the company is a separate individual, different from its shareholders, but owned by them. For hundreds of years this idea has held sway and in the majority of cases still dictates the actions of managers. When the compa-

## Our War Paradigm

nies are closely held by an individual or family, this mode of operation is understandable, but when we are dealing with a large corporation with its shares widely held and traded on the stock exchange, this concept of being a slave to the shareholders can no longer apply and in its place we have to start thinking of a company as a separate sentient being; an emancipated entity, in control of its own destiny. Shareholders are reduced to the status of investors who have very little say in what the company actually does.

The transition to this type of thinking is occurring slowly in the business world as mission statements are starting to reflect the idea of the stakeholder rather than the shareholder. In this way it is being recognized that there are interests other than the shareholder's that have to be considered.

But the war paradigm still reigns, it won't give up easily. The tendency to slowly evolve away from war can be reversed if the level of fear in the society rises. We are psychologically immersed in this war paradigm and automatically respond to fear by engaging in conflict. As the old threats (communism, the cold war, nuclear winter) decrease new ones take their place and we automatically propagate aggressive responses. Everyone wants peace, but we don't know how to achieve it. The contradiction involved in, "fighting for peace", seems lost on those most disturbed by the threats, and so the war paradigm continues with new enemies appearing whenever a slot needs to be filled.

The war paradigm perpetuates itself. It is a system designed for constant expansion and is tuned to pool the resources of the community under a central authority, principally to fight a war. Wherever it operates the rich get richer and the separation between the rich and the poor gets larger. When there are no wars to dissipate these resources, the economic growth eventually stagnates with some people having more money than they can spend and others not having enough to be self sufficient. Reinvestment, taxes, education and social services help to counteract this disparity in incomes, but these do not deal with the root problem.

The war psychology creates other social characteristics as well. It naturally leads to prejudice and

## Our War Paradigm

predisposes us to be aggressive to strangers. When exposed to an external threat the community comes together to fight. When there is no external threat it splits up into warring factions and the war activities continue internally. As long as the war psychology reigns we will find ways to fight and anyone recognizing this will conclude that we are naturally aggressive and pugnacious and that our future is very bleak.

If you believe that we are aggressive greedy creatures, only interested in our own self-fulfillment and uncaring of the plight of others, you are forced to predict a continuation of the war paradigm. On the other hand, if you accept that we are in fact creatures that are shaped by our social environment, and that we can slowly change to match the prevalent conditions, then you will wish to investigate how the environment has changed since the war religions were created. You would need to know where our natural instincts are taking us in response to these less hostile surroundings. The well-known Theory X and Theory Y of Douglas McGregor hits on this very point. Since he came up with these ideas in the 1950's behavioral scientists and businessmen have accepted the principle that people do not follow the pattern of Theory X behavior if they are treated in a humane way. Their Mr. Hyde emerges when they are threatened and their Dr. Jeckyll gradually reasserts itself when the threats disappear.

There is no denying that we can be and have been greedy and aggressive creatures, but instead of claiming that this is our natural state, we need to recognize that we can also be kind and generous. We need to examine the circumstances more closely and understand what makes us antisocial and what makes us human. I intend to convince you that, by studying the effects of fear on ourselves, we can understand why we became warlike and why we are now gradually growing out of this tendency. The repercussions of this are astounding.

The next step, I think, is to draw your attention to the effects of fear on ourselves. It takes no great intelligence to do this as we are well aware of these effects already. All we really have to do is to collect them together and look at them as an entity. Let me start by postulating a theory and defending it. This

## Our War Paradigm

style of "argument" is typical of our war paradigm. I put argument in inverted commas to draw your attention to a word which is used regularly in an inoffensive way, but which depicts conflict – and I do this to emphasis the idea that we live in a war paradigm.

If you agree that all our institutions are indeed war machines and that we train our children to fight, why do we get upset by gang warfare and crime? This behavior is just an extension of the same war philosophy. On the other hand, if we can redesign things so that we no longer have to think of ourselves as fighting and we can teach our children a different approach, what will happen to the wars in our society? Can we realistically predict a quantum leap in our quality of life? More on that later, first I need to focus your attention on a very limiting "judgmental" process that is implied by the war paradigm. This process was designed for a relatively simple society in which the main decisions to be made in relation to a stranger were: Are you friend or foe? Do you agree with me or do you oppose my views? Will you support me or will you fight me? Are you good or bad?

We have all been trained to assess each other on a good – bad scale. Is the person we have just met good or bad? Is their current behavior good or bad? This simple assessment process was a good way for a tribe to regulate their lives and accept only those who could be trusted to fight for the tribe in a war, but it has serious limitations in our modern world.

This simple binary assessment process gets complicated when we judge people's performance in the various roles they play in our more modern society. We can have a good policeman who is at the same time a bad husband, a good driver, a bad time keeper etc. We build up a matrix of good-bad characteristics which then defines the person for us and they then are given an overall evaluation of being a good person or a bad person. Having made that assessment, we react accordingly. Good behavior is accepted and invokes a positive response while bad behavior is frowned on and we demonstrate our hostility in some way. But the assessment is biased; just one bad characteristic can negate several good characteristics and make a person bad in our judgment. As we get to know more about the people we are in contact with it is likely that we will find some bad characteristic and we will classify them as bad. In such a classification system we inventively end up being surrounded by bad people.

We react with fear and hostility. Those around us sense our hostility and they respond in the same way. The level of fear in the community increases, stress increases, and the quality of life suffers. As each of us contribute to this communal fear and respond to it, the characteristics of the community are defined. Some communities have a very high ambient level of fear and react violently when things are changed (lynch the outlaw), while other communities, which have achieved much lower levels of fear, appear to be able to undergo change with little fanfare.

When you get sensitized to it, you can see the effects of fear in all aspects of human endeavor. Speaking to strangers may open you to a threat – so don't speak to strangers. Catching someone's eye

*Understanding Fear*

could lead to danger – so don't be caught looking at other people.

It is not traditional to examine our lives in terms of the fears that drive us, but join me on this adventure into the psychology of living and see the subject from a unique perspective. Instead of dividing the world into good and bad as we have traditionally done for at least the last 6,000 years we will look at people and their actions in terms of the fear that they are subjected to and how they respond to the threatening environment around them.

There is a social taboo about fear. We (especially men) are not supposed to admit to being affected by this emotion as it is traditionally considered "bad" to be subject to fear. It is easy to identify this as resulting in the need to have a social psychology that supports the brave warrior, but I urge you to break this taboo and admit to yourself that you, like everyone else, are subject to fear. This emotion is as natural as breathing and is essential for our continued well being as it ensures that we don't do foolish things, like walking in front of a bus. While we can normally manage the fear associated with finding our way through traffic, there are many situations that engender fear in us, a fear that would intimidate us or make us aggressive if we are unaware of its effects.

We must recognize when we are being threatened and manage our response to the fear this automatically generates. If we try to ignore it or pretend it is not there, or give into it and be either intimidated or aggressive, we are simply reacting to fear in a specific way and at the same time limiting ourselves to a reaction that may create rather than solve problems. We are designed with fear as a part of us and we cannot live without it. The infant that learns that the ground is painful if approached in a particular way needs to develop a fear of falling, but this fear must be controllable and must not lead to the infant being terrified of attempting to walk. Similarly, when we deal with social or spiritual fears we must also achieve a manageable level, if we are to choose our unique path through life and live the adventure.

# Chapter 2

# Social Responses to Fear

In order to control or manage anything we have to be able to measure it. With fear, this poses little difficulty as we are all well tuned to its measurement, and can easily train ourselves to recognize the signs which display the level of fear in the people around us.

Psychologists characterize our responses to fear as either "flight" or "fight", but there is much more to it than that. Much of our everyday behavior is prompted by some fear or other. We can measure fear by observing people's behavior and speculate on what fear caused them to behave in that way and then turn this technique on ourselves and measure our own stress or level of fear. There are many characteristic ways that people react to fear, some of these are listed below:

➢ **Ignore.** "That does not frighten me!" is a clear indicator that the person is affected by fear (frightened), but that they don't intend to be intimidated as, in their assessment, their goals are best served by not showing any weakness in the face of the threat. At this stage the person is probably not overwhelmed by the threat and can deal with the problem on a rational basis if they so choose. Unfortunately the reaction is seldom rational as we are trained to react aggressively to anything that upsets or threatens us. We feel that it is necessary to demonstrate our strength so that we are not taken advantage of.

➢ **Withdrawal.** We have all been there and done that. Confronted by an angry person, with overwhelming odds, or faced with a desperate situation with no path of escape we withdraw to our inner world and wait for the storm to pass. It can be voluntary, or it can develop to be an automatic reaction to any situation that looks threatening. This, like the other stereotyped responses listed here, sometimes evolves from childhood to become a characteristic of the person and form the basis of their response to any challenging situation. We have all met people who seem happy to withdraw from the world and live a quiet life placidly existing until the inevitable end. If it works for you, you may not want to change, as the alternatives seem too difficult or frightening or simply not desirable.

➢ **Submittal.** A dog will sometimes roll over on his back and offer a submitting stance to another dog. This tactic usually works as the aggressor seldom takes advantage of this vulnerability to press an attack. People also adopt this approach, but people are smarter than dogs and the aggressive person may interpret this as a tactic to gain control (they are threatened by this behavior) and may respond with violence. Submittal or silence is a favored tactic when someone feels that they are facing overwhelming odds. Employees facing their boss generally have no alternative when the boss gets angry and they adopt a submitting stance to ensure that their damage from the incident is minimized and a relationship which is important to them is maintained. Sometimes the submittal stance infuriates the aggressor who needs action to relieve his stress, or in other cases the aggressor is embarrassed by his actions and the submittal of the opposition amplifies this embarrassment and this results in the aggressor getting angrier and in some cases losing control. This is an example of where a control system fails, because the signals coming back do not have the intended effect.

➢ **Humor.** This is possibly the most complicated form of human behavior. It is often effectively used to reduce the level of fear in a group. If you can see the funny side of things it means that the situation is no longer threatening and you don't need to respond to the threat in the traditional way.

➢ **Action.** The fight or flight response is action which is traditionally associated with fear. There is a therapeutic value in action that reduces the level of fear. When a Hurricane is coming, those people who are actively preparing are in better control of their fear than those who sit and wait. Similarly, after the Hurricane passes through those who start immediately to rebuild their lives are in much better shape than those who sit and wait for help. Unemployed people get upset quickly as there is no mechanism that can be used to dissipate the stress. When large groups of people are affected by the same high stress situations, a march or some other non-violent action that demonstrates intent can be very therapeutic. The key is action. When you are in a stressful situation, action can help to reduce the level of fear. Unfortunately, in many cases we don't know what to do to relieve the stress and as a result we end up being withdrawn.

➤ **Bitch and moan.** This is not easily accepted as a reaction to fear, but you should recognize that people generally ignore the things that do not threaten them and by default, when something happens that threatens, they react by skillfully manipulating other people to gain control and so reduce the perceived threat. By complaining they feel that they are taking action to remedy the situation. Sometimes this evolves as a cultural characteristic. Radio call-in programs come to mind. It is easy to find fault with everything the politicians or businessmen do, to predict dire consequences, to insinuate nefarious practices, and to feel that you have achieved something, that you are somehow better off after doing this. In reality this behavior is a non productive response to a threat.

Like most reactions to fear, this behavior is addictive. Once someone starts the practice spreads and a general atmosphere of fear and dissatisfaction results. I have been part of companies where this attitude is prevalent, from the top management to the porter. Everyone feels that they are being taken advantage of and the company performs very poorly. It is an easy trap for monopolies to sustain as the normal process that the economic environment uses to get rid of these companies is blocked. Where there is competition, this acts to eliminate the weak and the environment gets cleaned up. However where this attitude becomes prevalent on a national scale, the whole society suffers and sometimes the economy collapses entirely.

In many homes this technique is used to relieve the stress of one of the partners while increasing the stress in the other. A typical situation would be the husband wanting to withdraw to recover from the stress of the day and the wife wanting to get things done around the house. Unfortunately neither understands that the other is reacting to fear and this lack of understanding results in continual:

> ➤ **Unbending focus.** Inability to shift focus from the one overriding problem facing them is one of the characteristics of a frightened person. When we detect this behavior we can immediately learn a lot about the individual's perception of their environment. The traumatized mother will not be interested in anything other than the recovery of her sick child. The business owner will be unable to concentrate on anything other than his failing business. When

someone nags and nags at a particular point, understand that they are terrified.

➢ **Anger.** When the level of fear gets high enough we sometimes react with anger. We have become angry because something has threatened us. This is a natural reaction and gives clues to the person's concerns, but it is also a well-worn path for manipulation. People respond to anger with fearful obedience. If you get angry the people you are dealing with will probably try to placate you by carrying out your orders. Because we are smart, we learn to use this technique to get our own way and for many people (it's quite obvious in some kids) it has become a method of manipulating those people they interface with on a regular basis while they demonstrate more civilized behavior to strangers. If they understood that their actions were driven by fear they might want to change.

➢ **Aggression.** Anger leads to aggression. It may be possible to be aggressive without being angry, but it certainly is much easier when you are angry. There are many clues which indicate that aggression results from fear (the fight or flight syndrome again) and a perceptive person will not find this concept difficult to accept. From the animal world, there are several examples of relatively tame animals turning aggressive when cornered. With no alternatives for survival, their level of fear escalates and they become aggressive.

Human beings also react with aggression when they feel that they have no alternative, but because this action is socially desirable in many circumstances, we go to elaborate means to create the conditions that make us aggressive. In the ancient world there are many recordings of leaders threatening their followers with instant death if they do not fight the enemy, while today we threaten employees with dismissal if they do not get their jobs done. "Meet your budget or you are fired" is a typical threat that is used to achieve aggression through increased fear.

Sometimes, when you are with a group of people you can feel the level of fear rising. It may be that someone has said something that everyone knows will produce a violent reaction from a member of the group, but it could also be triggered by a number of things. The fear seems to travel around the group like an electric current; there is energy in the air that is exhilarating. It is exciting, but dangerous (perhaps the two cannot be separated) and can easily result in violence. If it does, it is likely that the violence will escalate as fear has characteristics similar to that of fire and can easily spread and leave destruction in its path.

This violence is seldom physical: we are much too civilized for that. I am referring to violence through speech and body language. I have been to many directors meetings. Sometimes there is a lack of trust or respect for the other directors on the board. This comes out of a feeling that they may be using their position to further their personal interest or those of some other organization. When this lack of trust exists, the meetings become very inefficient. Any suggestion has to be examined from the point of view of how it may benefit a number of associated people and organizations. The discussion gets more emotional as the logic behind the decision gets too complicated to follow. In many cases this results in the board members making emotional rather than logical decisions.

This illustrates another characteristic of human behavior which we all know happens, but we have not related it to fear. Where the facts are known, we trust each other and the direction is clear, we can easily work together to come up with an optimum decision. We focus on the decisions to be made and stick with logic. The discussion flows. Ideas are judged on their merit. Different ideas are integrated to form an optimum path.

Contrast this with the normal decision making situation. The available information can be interpreted in a number of different ways. Various pet theories abound, each person argues for his own position. If blame is normally thrown around in the organization, each person positions himself or herself to avoid blame and direct it at others. They don't really trust each other and are not sure who they should cooperate with. In this scenario no one can accept anyone else's position as it may result in a disadvantage to him or her. The combination of the vague information, many possible interpretations, and the lack of trust result in a high level of fear and stress as the participants are conscious of the repercussions of making a bad decision and they don't feel comfortable with any suggestions other than their own. This is an extremely difficult decision making atmosphere and meetings generally end with the chairman having to impose a decision that the majority of people think is the wrong decision and with everyone stressed out.

> **Power.** Seeking power can also be viewed as a reaction to fear. We all seek power over our own lives, but a small portion of the population seeks power in the sense of having control over other people's lives. These power seekers do not generally exhibit the typical characteristics of a fearful person as they have learnt to channel their reaction to fear in a specific way. Several possibilities present themselves. The power seeker may be motivated by a fear that the community will be harmed – Winston Churchill during the second world war for example. Alternatively the power seeker may be fearful of someone attacking him and needs to feel in control of the people around him so that he can live

with some security. Name your favorite dictator as an example of this. These people need the reassurance that no-one is dissenting and react with extreme violence when this is not forthcoming. We often draw analogies between these neurotic power seekers and spoilt children. They require both constant assurance that they are in control and constant assurance that they are not threatened. Each order that is obeyed provides this reassurance.

In some cases these leaders, who have taken short cuts to get into power, become very lonely and isolated as they recognize their vulnerability and begin to be suspicious of those around them. They can then become unstable as they panic and start behaving irrationally as fear directs their actions and they seek more and more assurance that they are indeed in charge while destroying anyone who could possibly be a threat. Fear is the main reason for the saying "Power corrupts and absolute power …etc."

> **Greed.** The main reason for accumulating more than you can spend is to ensure that you will always be able to support yourself in a style

that you find acceptable. This need is derived from the fear that you will not have sufficient resources to sustain yourself. Greed and Power are very closely related and result when people react to fear in a specific way. It is commonly accepted that greed is what makes the capitalist system work. As greed is derived by fear, the real motivator is fear.

*Just as we have developed systems for managing greed, we can similarly manage fear*

When you see people seeking power and being greedy, how do you react? My guess is that a large part of the reactions can be classified under the heading: "fear and hostility". You either withdraw or get aggressive. I invite you to consider a different approach. Instead of reacting in the traditional way, try to understand what is driving the person to behave in the way they have. You know that it is driven by fear; all you need to do is to deduce what is behind that fear. Understand your environment (which increasingly means the people around you) and learn how you can cooperate with this environment to improve it. This simple change can alter your life and if enough people do it society will be radically altered for the better.

By knowing how we respond to fear we can learn how best to manage our lives and interface with others in a positive way. This is also an excellent means of discovering more about yourself. When you feel angry try to understand what has threatened you to produce this anger, and then see what you can do to manage the threat before you are forced into an aggressive response.

There is another way to look at the fear producing situations that we face daily. By grouping these into different categories we can more easily understand the forces acting on us and forming the stresses in our social environment. Stress is generated by fear and relieved by action. High stress results when we know that action is required to alleviate a fear, but action is blocked. We are either unable (unwilling) to take the necessary action or we are uncertain as to what action to take. The following illustrates increasingly stressful situations:

➢ **The action required is known and easily executed.** A simple example is crossing a single lane road with little traffic. We are aware of the danger and know how to avoid it. We have all the skills required and are not challenged to execute them. We can take immediate action to avoid any dangerous situation that may arise and very little stress results.

➢ **Several interrelated but easily executed actions are required.** The outcome depends on the level of skill and concentration applied. A game of Chess comes to mind. There are many different choices available. Skill and concentration is needed to play the game well. The level of stress depends on our relative level of skill and the consequences of the outcome. This approximates many real life situations. We have a multiplicity of easily executed actions which we can take to respond to a particular situation, but we are uncertain as to what action to take. This uncertainty results in lack of action an increased level of stress.

➢ **We know something is wrong but we don't know how to fix it.** We are forced to wait for help to arrive. Any action we think of is blocked by our uncertainty. The lack of action amplifies the stress generated by the situation. This could be a crisis that requires immediate action, like a medical emergency, or it could be a more long term problem like getting old or running out of savings with no prospect of earning more money. The inability to take action amplifies stress and can easily result in aggressive behavior.

➢ **Something might be wrong, we are not sure what and we don't know what to do.** A vague uneasiness prevails. More and more of the situations we find ourselves in in our modern world fall into this category. We are confused with conflicting information on what is good to eat, how many vitamin tablets to take, how much to eat, when to eat. Is the air polluted? What should we do about garbage? Is the Ozone layer disappearing? Are we wearing appropriate clothes for the occasion? Did we say the right thing? What can we say that would not cause offense or lead to a negative impression? How much time to allow for traffic delays? How can we please the boss? Our lives are filled with these types of situations, all of which are generated by fear and lead to stress because we are not sure how to deal with them.

We can all agree that the level of stress in our lives is increasing as we are bombarded with information that we don't have time to absorb and a range of choices which confuses. In more and more cases we are not sure how to deal with the situation. This fear-stress syndrome leads to withdrawal or to violent behavior. It is time to understand and manage fear.

By cutting and dicing the whole area of fear and examining it from different perspectives, we can radically improve our understanding of our social systems. This in turn opens the door to a very different society and indicates how we can get there with relative ease.

Like a typical engineer I want to develop a practical measurement system that I can use to evaluate what is happening. I want to be able to reduce my level of stress and control my reactions by understanding what is happening to me and the people around me. After years of being frustrated by my relationships with other people I decided to apply the training in problem solving, that I obtained while studying engineering, to the social scene. After several further years of struggling with this project I realized that I had to try to understand the impact of fear.

Since then the study of the dynamics of fear has been an exciting process with patterns emerging that relate closely to those that engineers have discovered when studying physical systems. The relationships

## Social Responses to Fear

are uncanny. It is the sort of thing that makes you wonder why it was not more widely understood.

I was introduced to the concepts behind feedback control systems at Sir George Williams University (now Concordia) in Montreal. I studied hard and made it through the filtering process into the third year of the program where we were introduced to Systems Dynamics and feedback control. I was captivated by this concept. In the labs where we used analogue computers to simulate physical systems, it was amazing to see an electrical circuit act out the response of a car's suspension system to a bump in the road. The circuit seemed to come alive when you introduced the feedback and I was deeply moved by the experience and speculated even then about the possibility of using this technology to understand economics.

Most people understand the concept of feedback control, even if they don't know it by that name. Everyone who drives a motor car uses it. You constantly look at the road and the traffic around you and use this information to control the vehicle you are driving. Your view of the road is the "feedback" in this control system. Your body uses feedback controls continually for its own internal systems. When you look at something and it appears blurred, your eye adjusts the lens to make as clear a picture as possible. When it is too bright or dark another feedback control system adjusts the size of the pupil. When you are hungry a control system sends a message to get you to eat, when your stomach is full you get another message to stop eating. When you get hot, a control system makes you sweat while taking other action to slow the generation of heat. There are many more of these systems in your body that measure a condition and seek to ensure that operations are contained within acceptable parameters.

In the social context, fear is the controlling mechanism. It is what we use to ensure that we don't damage ourselves physically and it also works very well in the mental realm, where we can talk of fear of the dark, fear of the unknown, fear of failure, fear of death, fear of losing money, fear of making this list of fears too long. There can be no doubt that we overwork fear in trying to control our society and we should be aware of a characteristic of control circuits which makes them go unstable when they are required to work outside their design limits.

A car in a skid is a good example of this. If the driver turns left and the car loses its grip on the road and continues going straight, the natural response of the driver is to turn further left. This results in the car going further out of control. The correct thing for the driver to do is to ensure that the tires regain traction before trying any further maneuvers, but often the response is fear driven. Instead of a cool rational approach, panic rules. This situation repeats itself over and over in our society and is the cause of much of our social stress. A few examples will illustrate the point.

There is an internally programmed mechanism in all of us which ensures that we want the best for our children. However, they resist our efforts to influence and guide them. This lack of response to our guidance is very similar to the car that goes into a skid and refuses to respond to the guidance of its driver. The inexperienced driver's response is the same in both cases, panic and a panic driven response, instead of the more effective controlled approach.

*Understanding Fear*

The parent should resist the tendency to panic and use force, but even when this is not possible, instead of becoming an autocratic "do what I tell you" type parent, they need to establish a dynamic relationship with their children. Explaining the effects of fear can help this process as they can feel its effects and see its effects in their parents. The child has to understand the dynamics of the situation and take their own path. The child has to develop the confidence to take the lead. If the parent keeps pushing and criticizing the relationship will suffer. A way of helping them develop confidence is essential.

On a wider scale, I see a repeat of the same process in the businesses with which I was associated. We are constantly looking for managers with drive and initiative, who are willing to take responsibility. And, at the same time, we are constantly destabilizing those individuals we have in management positions by challenging their self confidence, pointing out their failures and questioning their abilities. The reaction we get is very similar. Resistance, reluctance, withdrawal and a substantially reduced effort to communicate, followed by a much reduced output.

This slowing down is the natural consequence of not being able to deal with the fear that is unavoidably associated with getting things done in a fast-paced world. It is the ultimate response of any control system. When you are out of control just shut down and wait till things sort themselves out. While this may work with a car, on a national scale this results in high unemployment, high stress and high uncertainty. The level of fear rises and the country goes into economic decline.

Dealing with fear is not easy, there are a lot of skills to be developed, and these seem very difficult to acquire, but I would bet that when we have mastered them they will appear as natural as walking. But first we have to recognize the need for these skills by understanding the environment of fear that drives us. While it may be tempting to try to avoid this environment by eliminating emotion, this is not a solution that can be universally applied.

It is not sufficient to put emotions aside and deal only with a rational approach as, unfortunately, this seldom works. All of us have emotions and express these to a greater or lesser extent depending on our culture and our own highly individual approach to social situations. When someone with a strong rational bias is dealing with an individual who emotes to social situations, it becomes very difficult to communicate. Both individuals will become frustrated unless they have acquired the skills to overcome the hurdles that naturally arise. A rationalist who gets an emotional response is confused and seeks to deal with this confusion by applying logic and when this does not work he will tend to become angry and frustrated.

Similarly someone accustomed to a higher level of emotion will express this and feel rebuffed when the rationalist shows no emotional response. Many of our cultural dissimilarities evolve from different approaches to dealing with fear, not the least of which is the difficulties which arise between the male and female cultures in Western society. These are dramatized in "Men are from Mars, Women are from Venus" by John Gray.

We feel comfortable in our own particular emotional environment that has standard responses to social situations built into its fabric so that confusion, and the fear that results from this, is reduced to a minimum. Some cultures such as the male dominated Western business culture emphasize rationality as they see this as being best for business; contrarily, in the same Western culture, there are other communities, such as the performing arts, which rely heavily on emotionally laden communication.

On a larger scale, we can easily identify highly evolved rituals for fear management in all the major cultures. From this perspective, a culture appears to be an emotional nest, a familiar place in our mental realm which provides us with a relatively fear free environment by providing programmed rituals and responses to social situations. Some cultures have made these solemn and remote while others have made them hot with emotion.

Since starting to study fear I have come to the conclusion that all of our social interactions have a fear control component. The little things that we do every day, the way we dress, the please-thank you routines, the good mornings, the compliments, the talk about sports, the chit chat in the office, the radio stations, all help us to manage fear. We seem to need to have emotional strings attached to the people around us and we spend a lot of time and effort building and maintaining these connections as without them we very easily become frightened.

Let me point out how a word out of our war vocabulary so easily slips into our business lingo:

- Bullets, why do we call these bullets? Is it any thing to do with our war paradigm?

When I was in sixth form at Lodge School in Barbados and studying science for A-levels so that I could make an attempt at University, we spent some of our spare time debating religion. It was the usual thing, the professed non-believers, baited the firm believers who never seemed to be able to win an argument and always ended up with "you have to believe – you have to have faith". At Lodge we had what was called Seventh Period. These sessions were in the afternoon and sometimes a visitor would come into the class and talk to us about some subject or other.

One day Scratch, our head master, turned up with this guy who had turned religious while fighting in the war. After Scratch introduced him he did not seem to know what to say and asked if we had any questions, so I got up and asked him if he could explain what had happened to turn him into a Christian.

The speaker seemed quite pleased with the question and proceeded to explain how, while fighting in the war a bullet had hit his helmet at an angle which allowed it to penetrate through the metal, travel around the inside of the rim and destroy the lining, while avoiding contact with his head. This close call with death is typical of the experiences that convince people that God is looking after them. Unfortunately his story only confirmed my skepticism. From my very youthful perspective, the gentleman was obviously traumatized by the event and allowed this to influence his rationality. I don't know why this particular story stays vivid in my memory. Perhaps it is because he was trying so hard to convince me that God was real, but was having the opposite effect. He just convinced me that the trauma had removed his rationality. Fear at work again.

*Understanding Fear*

We had good fun with this in class over the following weeks as the believers thought they had won a minor coup and their opponents had to attack viciously to point out that the guy was demented. But the story was not unusual; there are many instances where people have become religiously inclined after a life-threatening situation. I believe that this is because of the programming that they receive when they are very young and which they return to when the level of fear becomes unbearable. It might or might not be as they claim.

Children have a hard time with this war paradigm. We try to raise them in a supportive environment at home and to a large extent this is achieved. We then send them to school, where they are exposed to a new environment that creates trauma – strange people, different races, hostile kids, foreign cultures, totally unexpected rules, deadlines, detentions, homework, and buses. The kids sometimes withdraw initially and then gradually crawl back out of their shells. The more sensitive they are, the longer it takes. While they are going through this process we send them to be confirmed into the church. There they are exposed to peculiarly dressed priests, awe inspiring buildings, and people speaking in hushed voices, praying and singing. The whole place is dominated by an overpowering statue of a man being crucified. As with school, it is easy to understand how this environment can also lead to trauma.

In church they are informed that they are guilty, that they were born guilty and cannot escape this guilt which is handed down from father to son, mother to daughter, ever since Adam and Eve were kicked out of the Garden of Eden. They learn that they are easily influenced by the devil and must watch for him at all times. They learn that there is a burning fire waiting for anyone who makes a mistake and transgresses God's laws. Once condemned to hell there is no escape and they burn for eternity.

They come out of the church and see their parents apparently breaking God's laws and they imagine God punishing them, sending them to burn in hell and leaving them, their poor children, alone in the world. This makes them become terrified and reacting to fear in normal human ways they blame their parents for the mess. They try to alter the behavior of their parents with little success. In some cases this results in a wall being erected between parent and child and the parent becomes guilty of passing on the guilt of the fall and the crucifixion, and guilty of not protecting their child by doing what the church instructs. In their terror the child can isolate themselves from their parents and the seeds of parent-child conflict are sewn.

Fear is a powerful tool and is most effective on the innocent, but while the trauma of the child is easily dramatized, the process is not unique and is repeated over and over in our social institutions. We learn to be very sensitive to the fear response as it is a good predictor of aggression. We learn to manipulate others using it – how to take advantage of a situation when we are in control, how to submit when we think that this is the better path – but from time to time we lose it, anger boils over, we throw caution to the wind and attack aggressively.

This sort of thing happens quite often, we watch it on TV and on the big screen; it is exciting when it does not overpower us. Many people tell of incidents which have made them so frightened that their rationality is chucked aside and a completely automatic fear response takes over. This is a good survival characteristic, but it leads to antisocial behavior.

When you think about it for a while you may conclude, as I have done, that fear is the root cause of all antisocial activity. Because of this we need to understand how it affects us. We need to model its behavior, or, more correctly, we need to model our behavior when we are under its influence.

# Chapter 3

# The Hierarchy of Fear

There are strong taboos against recognizing fear, and as a result of this we have gone to great trouble to develop our ideas of human behavior without mentioning the subject. We only recognize fear when it becomes overpowering. The behavior that results from overpowering fear is considered abnormal and the people that exhibit such behavior are generally taken out of circulation and ignored. But we should also recognize that normal people are affected by fear. It is by understanding the "normal" behavior that fear produces that we are able to manage it and effect the transition out of the war paradigm.

Abraham Maslow is mentioned in nearly every business course on human relations. His theory on motivation proposes that there is a hierarchy of needs and it lists human needs in an order that has food and shelter at the bottom and individual fulfillment at the top. He argued that the higher ranking needs only became relevant when the needs at a lower level are satisfied. At the lower end we are motivated by rewards which give us food and shelter while at the upper end we are motivated by our individual fulfillment.

A similar ordering of fears can be developed using the argument that when a person is in need of food and shelter, the fear of not having these is predominant and overrides any other fears that the person may have. Deprived of food and shelter, it can be expected that people will become angry and violent as this is a severe threat to their existence and gets them very frightened. Similarly, when these fears are placated, other fears become prominent and out of this concept a hierarchy of fear can be developed that closely follows Maslow's hierarchy of needs:

- ❖ **Spiritual.** It is difficult to rank this one as there are spiritual elements at work at all levels, but by including it here we can acknowledge its presence and accept that there are fears associated with the spiritual realm which impact heavily on our lives when we are threatened by unknown or uncontrollable elements in society. Under normal conditions spiritual fears lurk in the background and contribute to the overall level of fear maintained by each individual. As we get older the importance or impact of spiritual fears increases.

❖ **Food, Shelter and Health.** "A hungry man is an angry man!" When someone is hungry, and does not know where his next meal will come from, or if he has nowhere to live, it can be expected that these concerns will be paramount and will take precedence over all other fears. He may be forced to break social taboos and become violent or to take criminal actions to remedy the situation.

This brings one of our social dilemmas into focus as we do not have a reasonable way of remedying the situation where an individual does not have the means for basic self support. The immediate reaction of the war paradigm is that there is something wrong with that person and they should be shunned. The old tribal "exclusion of the misfit"

*The Hierarchy of Fear*

clicks in and the person is socially exorcised. Perhaps this is prompted by a long history of similar action when a tribe had to abandon their malformed or handicapped if they hoped to survive.

Despite much social progress, we still tend to think that anyone who is in this position has done something wrong to get there and should be avoided or punished. Fear of involvement also plays a part as well. We know that if we get close enough to the situation we will be drawn in and will probably be overwhelmed by the level of support needed. The easier approach is to pay your taxes and let someone else deal with the problem.

Notwithstanding this, a lot of effort (especially by the church) is put into trying to help the people who find themselves in this position, but it is seldom enough and a continual, apparently unresolvable, problem exists as the natural actions of our society forces people into this position on a regular basis. This is a direct result of our war paradigm and to solve the problem we have to recognize that it is driven by fear and learn how to manage it.

You can experiment with the effects of hunger on fear in your own home. Try to initiate a sensitive family discussion (the kids homework, keeping the house tidy, washing up, are all good topics) before a meal, measure the reaction, then repeat the experiment after a meal. I bet you will find that it is always more prudent to leave these discussions to the end of the meal when there is a much better chance of the subject being discussed without the hysterics that tend to be demonstrated when the family is hungry. This should help convince you that hunger has a big impact on people's behavior.

> ❖ **Safety and Security.** Stress has often been related to man's fight or flight reaction to perceived hostilities in the environment. In many cases confusion accompanies the fear as it is not clear that any specific action that the person can take will help the situation. In these circumstances, as no action can be taken to relieve the fear, this may lead to the withdrawal reaction mentioned above, but it can also lead to violence. If there are no threats relating to safety and security, or if these threats are not imminent, this fear has a lower priority and can be relatively easily set aside. However, if a severe

threat appears in this arena, we can expect that our concentration will be focused on it and we will not easily be diverted to other things.

- ❖ **Group Participation.** When we ostracize people we increase their level of fear. This is as true for a criminal in jail as it is for a new boy at school or a supervisor who has recently been promoted out of the ranks. Stress levels rise when they are no longer accepted as part of the familiar group. If an individual cannot (or does not) participate in group activities for whatever reason it can be expected that they will adopt antisocial behavioral characteristics. Participation in this context includes communication on items of fundamental importance to the individual, in a forum where they feel that they can express themselves without threat, and can receive accurate feedback from the group.

The opportunity to do this with non-family members does not normally exist outside of the work environment and this is one of the reasons that it is so essential to have a relatively fear free environment at work. When fear is maintained at a high level, the opportunity to make friendships and provide the nurturing that we all need seldom presents itself.

❖ **Self Esteem.** Without self-confidence, we rely completely on the opinions of others to measure our own worth. This makes us extremely vulnerable and we live in constant fear of being less than acceptable to our associates. This severely increases stress and limits our ability to participate socially as we are constantly interpreting the signals from the human environment around us to detect any negative indicators. Praise does wonders for these people, but only for a very short time as they adapt to praise and constantly need more. Those who achieve self confidence have a much more fulfilling life because they are not threatened when criticized. They either ignore criticism or use it as a means to facilitate their own evolution.

❖ **Self Realization.** When we have clear goals in mind and can measure progress easily, we have a quality of life that few achieve. Most people never get there and spend their lives following paths set for them by others and worrying about a host of miscellaneous things that become unimportant with the passage of time. Those who try to achieve self realization are plagued with the fundamental questions of life. Why are we here? How did we get here? Evolution or Creation? How best to live this life? Answers to these questions evolve from the analysis of fear on our lives. These are addressed later.

This hierarchy suggests that fear is a major source of antisocial behavior. People get antisocial when they experience a level of fear which moves them out of their rational capacity and into emotionally driven behavior. This may not result from any one major incident; it can be an accumulation of many minor setbacks. Sooner or later something happens that pushes them over the limit and antisocial actions result.

*Understanding Fear*

As we evolve away from the spiritual beliefs handed down to us, these no longer have the strength to assist us in managing fear. We can no longer have the assurance that the lord will provide. The need for an alternative fear management system is increasing.

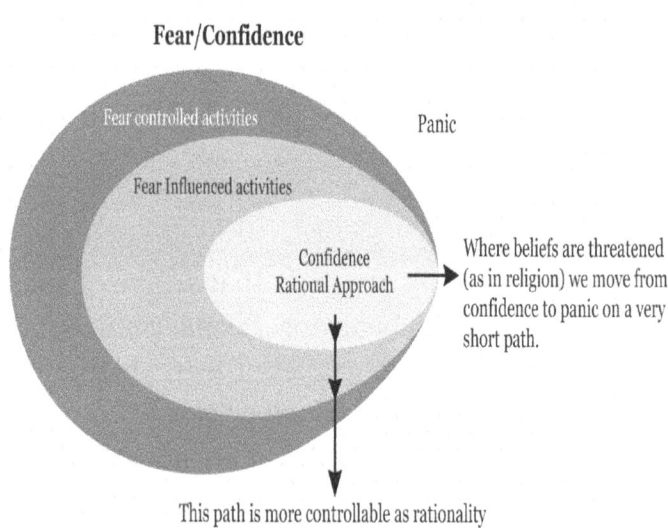

*The Hierarchy of Fear*

The diagram above illustrates the concept graphically. Most of us feel that we are operating in the center and are being rational, but we are wrong. Our rationality is based on a foundation of fear and there are many instances that illustrate this. Religious believers will argue rationally, but their entire arguments are based on fear driven assumptions. Our courts go to great lengths to follow the dictates of the law without realizing that this whole process of allocating blame is itself a response to fear.

It is very difficult to operate on a completely rational basis. This may not even be necessary or desirable. If we can understand that fear is a tool and needs to be understood and used wisely we can continue to live quite happily in the *fear influenced zone* while managing its inputs to our decision making processes. All of us have an optimum level of fear with which we feel comfortable. This is not a constant level, but varies depending on how strong we feel at a particular time. Many of our actions are guided by the subconsciously perceived gap between the level of fear that we are at and the optimum level for our current condition.

*Understanding Fear*

Suppose, for example you decide to visit a theme park with many different rides because you want to ride on a roller coaster. From the time the visit is planned, you will be anticipating taking rides. The expectation of fear will work you up to a state of excitement that will get stronger as the planned visit gets nearer. If you are part of a group of people planning to go on the same trip, as you talk about and plan the trip, your communication helps to reduce barriers and your friendship grows. (This technique is used to build teams, be it the experience of a wilderness trip for the business executives or the stress of boot camp for the army. It is all to do with fear. By introducing a common external fear, closer social interaction is achieved, the fear of each other is reduced and a team is formed.)

By the time you arrive at the park, you have built up expectations of a level of fear that you will experience that day and you are prepared to manage it and enjoy it. But there are many things that can go wrong. The level of excitement in the group may lead to quarrels that put a damper on the whole day. When you get a look at the roller coaster and hear the screams of the people riding on it you may be overcome by fear and decline to take the ride. You may not be feeling well that day or something may happen, such as problems at work, which introduce different fears and the sum effect of all the fears is that you are no longer interested in going to the theme park and would prefer to withdraw from everyone around you. On the other hand, if everything goes well and you have a successful day, you will then be in a good state of mind to deal with high levels of fear.

When we feel self confident and successful we can handle a high level of fear, but when we feel overcome and beaten we get stressed out very easily and cannot deal with minor incidents, especially those that we are close to and interact with in a highly emotional way. When you get home after having a bad day, and your ability to handle stress is very low, minor incidents take on major proportions and are likely to result in family squabbles. You may want to retire from the world and rebuild your shattered ego, but the kids are oblivious to this and scream for attention while your wife may be looking forward to you lifting her spirits after her difficult day.

*Understanding Fear*

If this only happens once in a while chances are you can deal with it. But repeated failures color our approach to life and gradually eat away at our ability to handle difficult situations. All of us are different and all of our approaches to fear management are unique. The more sensitive among us have a much more challenging time and experience wild swings in mood which are linked to our feelings of success or failure. Unfortunately, with the mind set and approach of our present society, these mood swings are emphasized by our self image. When we are down, we feel unsuccessful and unworthy and it is easy to conclude that we are unable to do any better. This mood leads to withdrawal and further failures. In this state of low spirits and frayed self image we tend to evaluate ourselves through the eyes of others. This in turn makes us very sensitive to what other people say about us while our feeling of failure makes us interpret what they say in the most negative way.

If we could get away from the over simplified good/bad self evaluation that our society encourages and move towards a more sophisticated understanding of the fear, we could approach life in a totally

*The Hierarchy of Fear*

different way. Instead of feeling sorry for ourselves when we are down, we can use the experience to increase our self-understanding; probe and find out why you are feeling down. This enhanced knowledge can then lead to skills that allow us to deal more effectively with the situations that develop around us.

In an average day, each of us deals with a wide range of fear-producing situations. Sometimes the level of fear gets too high for us and we feel stressed out or become withdrawn and unable to respond positively. Alternatively we may allow ourselves to get angry and control the fear in that way. Expressing anger is an effective fear control technique, but unfortunately it is usually associated with a loss of control and this reduces its productive impact. At the same time it must be recognized that controlled anger and aggression is a very effective tool for getting things done. However, if it intimidates those you are interfacing with, you can expect that communication will become very strained and even if they don't confront you, they will show their displeasure in a number of alternative ways. This is especially important in the Caribbean context as we have developed a high sensitivity to the whims and fancies of people in authority and the skill to tell them what they want to hear, rather than what we think. While this is a good technique for individual self-preservation, it does not contribute to a dynamic social development and the whole society suffers in the long run.

Much of the fear we live with comes from not knowing what to do. The modern world overwhelms us with choice and in many cases we don't have a reliable means of making the right selection. This encourages us to find a leader to follow and is probably one of the factors behind the prevalence of sports super heroes. Trained as we are to follow, we search for leaders and as the traditional sources for these loose prominence, others emerge to fill the need. We can see the effect of these super heroes on our youth. This is not a new phenomenon, simply an old pattern with new people playing the prominent roles.

> Because of this uncertainty of what to do, we have a strong tendency to follow the behavioral patterns of our leaders. Unquestioningly we

assume that whatever they do is right and as this behavior obviously worked for them, we assume it will also work for us. If the leader is a military figure who got power through armed rebellion, we can expect that this pattern of behavior will be reflected through the society. Children will act out the ritual of armed rebellion in play. Business leaders will be autocratic as will Union bosses and everyone who has to provide leadership.

➢ If the leaders gained their position because they have formed a powerful cartel with contacts in the right places this pattern is also repeated through the society with various groups staking out territory and achieving dominance in their own little kingdom.

➢ There is no question about the presence of war. It clearly exists in politics, as it does in organized crime. The difference is the way this power is maintained and how leaders are selected. Great ingenuity has been demonstrated in the way that society has migrated away from armed conflict while maintaining the war mentality. It shows how clever we are.

I invite you to mull over the things that bother you and come up with prescriptions for action. If these are violent, chances are that you are threatened by the situation. At the other extreme you could decide to close all mental doors and retire from the world. This is another typical reaction to overwhelming fear. Neither of these approaches is very effective. What is required is a process of reducing the level of fear. The warring parties have to be able to see their opponents as people like themselves, and understand that both sides are being driven by fear.

Before trying to mediate in disputes with this approach, be warned that frightened people do not listen to reason and your first step will have to be in the direction of dissipating the fears of the parties and moving them up the hierarchy of fear to the point of self realization.

This approach has major implications for a large area of society including our treatment of the unemployed and those guilty of committing crimes.

*The Hierarchy of Fear*

Examining our approach to justice helps to illustrate the differences that might arise out of this analysis in comparison to that practiced in our present society that is keyed to the good-bad analysis.

We have all experienced a lifetime of fear and it has shaped our character. It has given us our prejudices, determined if we will be aggressive or reclusive in response to various levels of fear, and colored our opinions of those we come into contact with. It also dictates how we will interface with them and how this interface will be governed by our prejudices.

Prejudices are formed when we make a formula. We have gathered some information and have linked various characteristics together in a cause and effect formula. Suppose, through our information gathering, we determine that every time someone is going to give us bad news they tense their body. We make up our formula by linking the body language and the bad news. To state the same thing in different words, we develop the prejudice that this body language is a precursor to bad news and we prepare ourselves for the bad news. We react to tension by getting tense ourselves.

*Understanding Fear*

If there is a lot of fear associated with the prejudice we panic and get locked into a very fixed, closed loop, where we can only focus on one thing. Because of the high level of fear we can't apply rationality to the situation as this is blocked by fear. When this happens, there is very little we can do about it, we don't question our response and we don't appreciate anyone else highlighting its irrational aspects, as this is embarrassing. Racial prejudice falls into this category. We have a natural fear of strangers that is emphasized by differences of appearance and culture. But we don't think that it is socially acceptable to acknowledge this fear so we pretend that it does not exist. We bury it. Cover it over, dance around it with social rules. But it does not go away and from time to time we realize that we are prejudice. This eats away at our self-confidence and keeps us from building self confidence.

There are many social situations that are so ticklish that it is acceptable to avoid the topic all together. We are all aware of our friend's sensitivities and use our social skills to tiptoe around them. At the same time we don't question our own, because it does not occur to us that this is something

*The Hierarchy of Fear*

that should be questioned. If we did, we would have a much better knowledge of ourselves, but we hide from this as well as we expect to be disappointed. Thousands of years of belief that we are horrible creatures helps to create this expectation.

The hierarchy of fears is a useful tool for analysis, and as we get skilled at this we will be able to start a serious self-examination. Contrary to the belief that we are mean and vicious, we will find that we are intelligent and sensitive social creatures who respond with violence when threatened. This analysis will also lead to the development of enhanced social skills and to the ability to more effectively deal with the difficult situations that arise from time to time in our relationships with others.

# Chapter 4

# Fearful Myths

Most of the criticism of our society is not helpful in trying to deal with its problems. This is because it usually seeks someone to blame. Having identified the culprits, we are drawn into the trap of thinking that we can solve our problems by punishing those identified as responsible. We spend a lot of time and effort doing this and its lack of success is accepted as inevitable because we believe that people are intrinsically selfish and bad. At the same time we have little confidence in the people entrusted with the job of punishing and expect that this job will not be done properly.

Our judicial system is based on the Christian myth that men are weak and easily influenced to do evil. Because of this belief, it is assumed that a high level of fear has to be maintained in society so that the temptations we face are balanced by fear of the consequences that will befall the perpetrator of evil deeds. By punishing those that don't conform to our social norms, we think that we are doing the "right" thing. It is a simple concept based on the myth that God is fighting the devil, and out of it falls the system of punishment that is handed out to those found guilty of crimes. Just as the biblical God punishes man for his misdeeds, so too should our leaders, and others in authority, punish those under them in the hierarchy. Priest punishes parishioner, boss punishes employee, judge punishes prisoner, wife punishes children and, too often, husband punishes wife and children with the use of excessive force. All of this is driven by fear. The leaders get worried when the followers do not demonstrate their willingness to follow. They then respond to this fear with the violence they think is necessary to ensure that socially accepted norms are maintained. They feel that if they don't do this, their position and the whole of society will be threatened.

We believe that unless rigid controls are maintained that our society will be reduced to havoc. Because of this we have restrained ourselves by erecting walls of fear around us that are enforced through the use of socially accepted violence. But by constantly reinforcing these beliefs we maintain a social environment that reduces our self-confidence to a minimum. This low self opinion makes us suspicious of others while enhancing our susceptibility to derogatory comments, and it forces us to be very aggressive when something happens which would indicate that "wrong" has been done. We rush to defend ourselves (our society) against this wrong.

Again, one of the closed loops of the war paradigm illustrates itself: Low self esteem producing high sensitivity, producing fear, producing aggression, producing war. The need to fight a war then creates a requirement for absolute control that is best achieved by robbing people of their self-esteem so that they can easily be manipulated for the betterment of the society. In this way, the war paradigm sustains itself.

Another of the underlying myths propagated by the idea of an almighty God is illustrated in the way the system of Justice decides what is right and what is wrong. Precedent, the idea that the decisions of the courts have to be based on what has gone before, is derived from the religious concept that the laws were handed down to man from God in ancient times and we should therefore follow the examples set by the ancients in deciding what we should do in the present. In this way we will be following God's instructions.

This is like trying to walk a straight line in a desert by sticking stakes in the ground and lining them up so that you can see your trail and so maintain a straight line. Unfortunately this means that we must proceed forward while looking back. This is what the Judicial System is doing with the idea of precedent. It seems to be more concerned about maintaining a straight line than trying to decide where we want to go and how best to get there. Again, fear shows its face. It is much easier (less frightening) to follow the example of what has gone before than to create a new direction. Even if a judge had the courage do this, there is no support mechanism, no means of ensuring that the community participates in deciding where they would like to go.

This effectively blocks any attempt to change the system that plods along with dinosaur-like fatality perhaps to the same end. This happens because, in a fear filled atmosphere, efforts to change things generate more fear. This then induces a strong tendency to stick with the familiar. The fear activated controls force the system to reject change. "Better to live with the devil you know than the one you don't" summarizes this approach. Without goals that motivate change, the judicial system remains in a stable, slowly evolving, environment that lags far behind the social needs generated by a society that has substantially increased its rate of change. This lack of goals has much wider implications.

Perhaps the most significant factor that comes out of the religious programming is the belief that we don't need goals as there is a precedent for this as well – God told us what to do in the Bible – all we have to do is to follow his instructions; just like the judges we look to the past for direction into the future. In this way the concept of precedent overshadows all of our planning. Instead of trying to decide what we really want to do, we concentrate on looking back and trying to ensure that where the pegs look out of line, we take corrective action to make them straight again. Where this process is taking us does not seem important enough to warrant examination as we are convinced that our all-mighty God has taken care of this and all we need to do is follow his instructions no matter how confusing or inappropriate these may seem to be.

This is another of the down sides of believing that an all-powerful God is in charge. It is like selling yourself to a fief or warlord. You give up your freedom to gain security. You don't have to worry about where you are going because your lord makes those decisions. But to maintain this security you have to keep up regular payments through servitude. If you think it through, this security is not worth the price. Because we typically follow patterns, as long as we are prepared to be subservient to God, we will also be subservient to other people in authority and we will live a life shackled to "mental chains".

It is much better to develop the skills needed to face the fear without the help of an all-powerful God. Instead of relying on God, or his priests, for directions, we need to use our own intelligence and make the best decision we can. Then we learn; then we get our freedom along with the additional responsibility. This of course adds fear as making our own decisions on the direction of our life is a very traumatic thing.

The hierarchy of fears listed above suggests that we are shaped by our environment. Given the opportunity, we will do what we can to better ourselves. With this starting point we would approach justice in quite a different manner. We would have to conclude that people commit crimes in response to fear. To minimize antisocial behavior we would then want to do two things. 1) Erect barriers of fear against antisocial behavior, as we presently have, and 2) Remove the threats that force this type of behavior. It is this second step that will produce the biggest results and create a quantum leap in the quality of life.

If you are convinced that man is basically bad, you may think that this approach is unattainable, but Steven Covy (Author of "The Seven Habits of Highly Effective People") has attracted much attention by emphasizing that we have to be true to ourselves if we wish to enjoy a higher quality of life. Once we can get to manage fear we will find that there is an internal control system that ensures that we become civilized.

*Fearful Myths*

Where poverty or famine is a real threat we can understand that people respond to this environment by hoarding food and being very selfish. But the affluent societies also hoard resources. This takes the form of excessively high salaries, profits, savings or other accumulations of wealth. This social behavior tells us that although some individuals in the society may have lifted themselves to higher levels, the society as a whole is still quite low on this hierarchy of fear and promotes this behavior. It continues to do this despite the predictions of the economic model which indicates that, the more evenly wealth is distributed, the better off everyone is.

When solid, well established theory is not accepted, we can conclude that we are not behaving rationally. This irrational behavior is prompted by fear. We do not accept the theory because we are frightened that if we change our present system we will be worse off. The failed experiments with socialism and communism support this concern while our spiritual beliefs make us very suspicious of such a fundamental change.

*Understanding Fear*

For many eons, wealth has been associated with being blessed by God while being poor was seen as an outward indication of God's disapproval. We have used this concept to stigmatize the poor and ostracize them from the rest of society, believing that they have brought their condition on themselves by not exhibiting the true Christian characteristics of hard work and thrifty spending. It is easy to believe that God has punished these people. For our part, we should not oppose the will of our maker. Here we are caught in one of the many contradictions of the war paradigm where our natural tendencies to give are curtailed by fear and suspicion. We expect that there will be people in society who will take advantage of any generosity and this, along with the conviction that some people should be poor and will always be poor, restricts our instinct to share. We solve this problem by giving an occasional donation while leaving the bigger problem in the hands of higher authorities.

As we move away from the influence of these ancient ideas, we can more easily address these social problems in a rational way. This is leading to the realization that prison reform programs are essential, as are skills training for the poor. The now famous "give a man bread and you feed him for a day, teach a man to make bread and you feed him for life" along with the realization that the best method of population control is education are concepts that are replacing the older "give alms to the poor". This more enlightened approach is welcome, but it is only a start. There is much more change to follow as more and more of the socially accepted myths based on the old religious beliefs fade away under the scrutiny of clear headed analysis.

We are slowly discovering that, apart from this social pressure to hoard and seek power, an affluent society will happily live within socially acceptable norms without the threat of punishment to keep them in line. In Western societies it has become accepted behavior to fight over resources at work, but to demonstrate lavish generosity outside of the work environment. This seems to demonstrate that we are conscious of living in two paradigms. The rules of the war paradigm apply at work while more civilized rules govern the rest of our lives. Unfortunately this leads to social confusion as the rules for the two paradigms get mixed up from time to time and it is never very clear which rules should apply.

From the point of view of the fear analysis, this judicial system generates several clues as to the fears that drive society and the techniques used to control society. It illustrates:

- Fear of the devil (or the temptation to do evil deeds) and the control technique of balancing this with the fear of punishment, so that we can feel assured that we are protected from this temptation while we go about our normal daily lives.

- Fear of confrontation and the control method of designating specific people who's duty it is to confront (police, lawyers) and the use of ritual (laws, the court room procedures, judges in specific dress etc.) to reduce fear. The use of ritual in this way is a theme which is repeated constantly in our society.

*Fearful Myths*

- Fear of the future and the tendency to look to the past, instead of to our goals, when making decisions about the future.

- Fear of social misfits and the tendency to exclude them from society.

The private sector is another area where the concepts originally developed for fighting have been adapted to modern business and in this way several myths have been propagated. Let me briefly outline two features of this, the organizational structure and the concept of service to the organization.

The Egyptians created the oldest and most successful civilizations in the Fertile Crescent and their philosophy is found in many of the other civilizations that emerged in the Middle East. One notable feature of the Egyptian civilization is their pyramids. They have spent much time and effort building pyramids, not only physical pyramids, but social organizations based on the same concept. They must have thought that they had discovered a fundamental law when they came up with the idea of the pyramid. This same pyramid structure is still

*Understanding Fear*

with us today in nearly all of our social organizations both physical and spiritual.

I understand that heaven is organized into different ranks of angels with God and his son Jesus forming the top layer of that pyramid with progressively lower ranks of angels under them. Here on earth our churches are organized similarly with Pope, Arch Bishop, or Reagent, playing the leading role and other lesser officials forming the lower ranks. In business we have a pyramid structure with various levels of bosses while in politics and government there are similar hierarchical ranking systems. This structure is so ingrained in our psyche that we don't question the need for it. We accept that someone has to be the boss and we automatically form the pyramid structure whenever something has to be organized. The main reason this works is its efficient command structure, but it has its limitations.

Because these organizations are so similar, our expectations of what a Boss (the person at the top of the pyramid) should do are consistent with the behavior of the more outstanding members of that fraternity. The most publicized figure is of course the

War God of Biblical fame and so it is expected that all other bosses will follow the pattern of behavior established by this most notable character. It is expected therefore that the Boss of a company, or any of the intermediate bosses, will be autocratic and cruel and keep all the information they can away from their subordinates. Instructions will be very limited and veiled in mystery. Large penalties will be imposed on anyone making mistakes. Those that fail to comply will be banished from the kingdom and left to their own devices. The Boss does not bother himself with the methods used to achieve compliance with his instructions, this is left to the intermediate bosses who have a lot of freedom to develop their own way of doing things, but who generally copy the behavioral characteristics of the ultimate Boss.

This biblical Old Testament approach to leadership was eventually labeled Theory X behavior by Douglas McGregor in his ground breaking work published in the 1950's. Much progress has been made in this field since then, but prior to that, the primary human relations manual for business leaders was the Bible and it is this influence that was the driving force behind the management attitudes that powered the industrial revolution.

Please don't think that I am blaming anyone for this. It is simply the history of a people driven by fear and demonstrates their attempts to minimize this fear by following the directions of their God. The leaders were merely doing what they thought was best at the time and were acting out the expectations of the society as a whole. This expectation was carefully cultivated by the Church, which itself was grappling with its own fears and going to great lengths to ensure that their God was being served in accordance with his expectations. Out of this fear-drenched atmosphere came the Protestant Ethic that is recognized as the spirit of Capitalism.

Our present day work ethic has evolved from this and is essentially the expectation that workers will follow their instructions and give their best while accepting a very low wage without complaint. These roles of Boss and servant were well defined in the religious texts and for a long time were accepted as the proper way to behave. No one dared to step out of line as this could be expected to produce a fate worse than death. At the same time, poverty forced people to steal and so provided evidence that people are intrinsically evil (these actions could be thought of as 'the work of the devil' and they thereby helped to reinforce the religious teachings). In this environment it was very obvious that rich people were good and poor people were bad.

Service to the organization, something we still celebrate, is a relic of this system which was developed to fight wars and then evolved to be the backbone of the private sector. This distinction between the good and the bad, the rich and the poor, separated society.

This tendency to divide society into different groups, label them and then treat them with prejudicial behavior comes out of the We-They approach that is handed down from the Jewish religion. In a fear-laden atmosphere, anyone who looks, acts or speaks differently is subject to suspicion. Racial and social prejudice comes from fear generated by this difference. It is a good survival tool when you are surrounded by enemies who are bent on your destruction.

The fear and the prejudicial behavior continue into our more enlightened societies because we have put a taboo on fear and refuse to acknowledge its presence. Instead of understanding the reasons why people are prejudiced, we adopt the typical war paradigm approach and label them "bad" and then adopt our own prejudicial behavior towards them. One of the most popular stances in the Caribbean today is to be prejudiced against prejudiced people. I can't see that this is leading to a solution.

These ideas generated at the time of the "fall" are so embedded in our social genetic code that we automatically assume that they are an essential part of human nature. We firmly believe that we are by nature aggressive, greedy, cruel, self-centered, uncaring of others, antisocial, paranoid...there are many more I could add, but you get the picture. We assume that this is our natural state and we have to go to great lengths and solicit the aid of God to be able to rise above this natural state, while fully anticipating that even with the help of God, we will find that this effort is burdensome and very difficult to maintain.

But let me pose a different hypothesis, one that not only matches the observations, but helps to predict behavior and gives us a tool which we can use to influence our own and other people's behavior. It is a very simple statement, but it has a lot of meat in it:

## Our social behavior is shaped by our social environment

By social behavior, I mean the way we behave in relation to each other. If I am in an environment in which I have to fight for food, then that is what I will do. If food is not a problem, then my next priority is shelter. If there are alternative ways of getting these things I will use them and avoid fighting and stealing. If I started out stealing food and then food became abundantly available, I might continue to steal long after I have enough because I am now trained to steal. I have developed the technical and social skills to steal. I then apply these skills to everything else that I do. This is the way our society has evolved. As the environment changes, the society responds, but with a time lag which results in our retaining antisocial behavior long after it is no longer a necessary part of survival.

*Understanding Fear*

Understanding that people's aggressive behavior is driven by fear reveals a different world. This insight leads to a quantum leap in our ability to move out of the war paradigm. Everything that we do is reflective of the fears we have. Our actions are a clear indicator that can be used to understand our behavior. Try this approach with some of the significant events in your life. Look back at those events that stand out in your past and ask: What fear drove you at that time?

Sometimes it is very difficult to explore your past in this way. There are things buried there that you don't want to expose. You have buried them because you don't want to appear bad to yourself. Now you must abandon this good/bad paradigm and understand that you are driven by fear and there is no point blaming yourself for being frightened.

Fear makes us judgmental. Every time you use the word good or bad it indicates that you have made a value judgment and you should realize that this value judgment is a product of the war paradigm that we have to move away from. Instead of being judgmental adopt a different approach and understand that:

## Our actions are not good or bad; they are simply indicators of the nature and level of our fears

Children learn a lot from their parents. Not only from what they are told, but also from the way they act. Kids are very keen observers and easily detect all the subtle social indicators that tell them how their parents react to their environment. They get their status in the society by sensing how the people around them interact with their parents and they read the nuances of the family conversation and use this as a guide to the value judgments that they make. They also copy behavior much to the embarrassment of their parents.

There is a social stigma about fear. Admitting that you are afraid is like admitting that you have AIDS. No one wants to listen, they prefer to ignore you, make you invisible, so that this horrible thing does not have to be faced. I have been to management meetings where the managers are very frightened by the threats of the Union and react violently. I have been to staff meetings where things get so tense that you can feel the atmosphere crackle. The managers are tense, the staff are tense, and instead of dealing with the issues that the meeting is called to address, it gets very emotional and degenerates into a lynching mob. The leaders are blamed for everything that has gone wrong. They, in turn, blame the staff. I have been to political meetings where the politicians on the platform try to blame white people for every wrong in the society. All this is not good behavior or bad behavior it is the normal behavior of frightened people. It is people responding to their environment. We have to break the loop, recognize that we are simply responding to fear and take corrective action.

We often react to crisis by trying to decide who was right and who was wrong, but the issue is not one of right and wrong. Establishing blame is not a productive activity. The real issue is how to repair the damage and try to ensure that it is not repeated. You may argue that this is what we are trying to do when we establish who is right and who is wrong as we can then punish who is wrong and this will prevent the reoccurrence of the crisis. But this is a weak argument and can only apply in a limited number of very well defined circumstances. The more practical problems like how do we get ourselves out of an economic crisis, or how are we going to increase employment, or eliminate poverty are not solved by blaming someone. In fact the process of establishing blame results in increased fear, anger and divisions in society which increases rather than reduces the problems.

The further away from an event you are the bigger it becomes, and as long as we refuse to question the bible stories that are relayed to us through the very distorting media of people's memories, translations and imaginations, we will remain bound by our mental chains. The power of these stories will not diminish until we question them and read around the events to understand the environment that produced them. Until we do that we will be living in fear of an unknown element that exists only in our minds.

Take Exodus for instance. This is the story of a man trying to get his people to leave a relatively comfortable environment and go into the desert. To achieve this he utilizes the idea of a very powerful God and he has to use all the means at his disposal to show that this God is more powerful than the other gods and that he is the personal God of the tribe. You need to remember that the Bible was not written down until around 800 BC so this event that is described in the second book of the Bible took place 400 years before the Bible was written. This is sufficient time for storytellers to convert ordinary men into heroes and to introduce God's directions into all decisions. It shows how clever Moses and the other leaders were in countering the fear of leaving Egypt with the more powerful fear of God.

The rituals and covenants which are described in Exodus illustrate a technique for fear management. These stories and rituals constantly reestablish belief or faith, and the other trappings of the religion are there to reinforce this faith. This faith, or absolute conviction, is the most important element in fear management that I have ever come across.

But blame is not helpful; it only frustrates and robs energy. Moses did not blame the Egyptians and encourage the Jews to wallow in a pit of self-pity; instead he got on with the difficult job of establishing an identity that bound the group of people together and gave them faith in themselves. This is a lesson to be learnt from Exodus.

Suppose Moses had not kicked out the Golden Calf and had continued to worship this now foreign God? What would have happened to the Jews? I am sure that anyone who has studied the impact of religion on people's destiny will agree that they would never have accomplished nearly as much as they have.

The Christians went to great efforts to transform this Jewish God and make him their own. To achieve this they had to show that the Jews had lost their exclusivity and the Jesus story is used extensively in this way. Just as Moses had to kick out the Golden Calf, the warlike God of the Old Testament had to be reformed. The idea that a race is chosen by God and thereby has some advantage over another race is no more than a rerun at this stage. A completely new idea is needed, something that can capture our imaginations, help us manage our fear and develop the skills we need to work and live together with a higher level of harmony than has been possible in the past.

*Understanding Fear*

If we are going to move away from the good/bad approach, we need to understand that it is not going to be productive to argue about the past, to establish who was right or wrong or if the Church was a good influence or a bad influence. Instead we have to try to understand why people did the things that they did and how they used the tools at their disposal to achieve their objectives. Using this approach, we can look at religion as a tool that was invented for one purpose and evolved to be used for many others. It is a product of the social environment.

The relationship between strong religious views and the trouble spots in the world is quite apparent. Northern Ireland with their Catholics and Protestants and the various countries where there is strain between Muslims and Christians are often cited as cases that indicate that religious beliefs cause strife between people. But there are also many regions where different religious beliefs exist quite peacefully side by side and the religious leaders actively promote tolerance, so there must be some other explanation for the strife – it cannot be religion that causes it. A closer examination of the situations indicates that there is an underlying conflict that results in an escalation of fear. This heightened fear makes people turn to their religious institutions for support and it is the chemical reaction between the war religions and fear that produces the social dynamite. Religions were designed to help people fight and they do this very well.

As tensions rise the tendencies to see the enemy as evil increase. Statements by the opposing faction are automatically considered to be lies – propaganda that is of the enemy's arsenal. Their response is to block all communication, negate all arguments, sew distrust and do violence to their critics. They give no quarter and in addition to extreme aggression and courage in battle they also try to wipe out their enemies, remove them from the face of the earth, eradicate them and their families, and ensure that they are completely annihilated. While doing this, they are convinced that they are doing God's work. There is no stopping this terror driven activity as the violence induces more fear and a firestorm of fear and violence results.

Biblical references are drawn and examples of previous occasions where God has done violence to the enemy are used to justify this inhuman behavior. This is something in which religion excels. The process for doing it is filled with opportunities for the current social environment to influence the process. When the environment is hostile and threatening it can be expected that this fear-laden atmosphere will produce bellicose messages from the ultimate authority.

So don't blame the leaders, don't blame religion, don't blame the opposition, don't blame the enemies, just understand that they are scared and are dealing with frightened people. Before any progress can be made towards peace, the level of fear has to be reduced. Only after this level has become manageable is there any possibility that logic can be applied to the situation.

## *This is the road to freedom*

We all wish for freedom, but most of us interpret this to mean, freedom to be close-minded. When we talk of freedom of religion this is in effect what we are saying and we don't follow through the logic of the situation sufficiently to understand the contradiction of it. If we are happy for different religious views to exist, we have to anticipate that when situations arise which heighten the level of fear that society will break along the lines created by these differences of opinions. If we want to build a strong society, we have to have freedom to be open-minded. This does not mean that some of us will be open minded, it means that we have to develop social systems that ensure that everyone is open-minded, but this is in itself very difficult. If you use force, then a police state is created. We have to use education and persuasion. If we educated based on racial or religious prejudices, we are merely perpetuating the status quo. This emphasizes the importance of ensuring that we have a rational basis for what we teach.

Everyone has their favorite fears and belief systems; we hang onto these for dear life. We will discuss these with apparent open-mindedness and will apply logic to reinforce our beliefs and to convince others that these beliefs are reasonable and logical. But when the logic points to something that threatens, we will quickly transfer responsibility to a higher authority, one which is beyond our comprehension, thus avoiding any further questioning. In this way the different beliefs are maintained and instead of evolving as a unit, society maintains its divisions.

The only road to freedom is through fear management. Attempts to achieve unity through force have all failed as *the application of force increases the level of fear and this automatically resists the change.* When a community unites simply because of the threat of a neighbor, the unity does not outlast the threat as the fundamental causes of the differences still exist.

Socialism, and its extreme version Communism, were well meant attempts to achieve unity of purpose, but unfortunately the people who conceptualized the idea did not anticipate that the leaders would be overcome by fear and turned into despots. Establishing rule by force did not work. Socialism is a great idea, if it had worked it would have managed a lot of our fears, but for it to work we have to be able to achieve the necessary unity by desire rather than by force.

*Fearful Myths*

If the communist ideas could have been executed by agreement rather than by massive use of force it might have worked. But the timing was wrong. You can't move out of the war paradigm when war is a real threat and everyone is terrified. I would argue that the movement failed, not so much because it was a bad idea, but because its leaders could not take the pressure. They could not handle the criticism. They panicked and instituted a police state rather than risk losing power. This is where they made their mistake and lost control of the whole movement.

However, the attempt has taught us many things. It shows that there are many well-intended people who yearn to help their fellow man, but that this help is difficult to give as any change from the expected normal way of doing things generates a high level of fear. This acts like an inertia or friction that resists the change. If the leaders panic and respond to this with massive force, fear escalates and the resistance goes underground, communication is turned off, suspicion and hostility reign. This in turn frightens the leaders who then step up their strong-arm tactics and the fear cycle feeds on itself.

*Understanding Fear*

Fear generates fear until it is beyond the control of anyone and society kills itself.

It can happen in any society, the McCarthy era in the USA, when prominent citizens were attacked for supposed beliefs in Communism is another example of fear at work. Although McCarthy championed the cause, there must have been an underlying fear of Communism in the society that allowed this campaign to work. Again the same pattern emerges. I don't think that McCarthy was evil, nor were the people he attacked evil, it is just that they were facing a major challenge to their way of life from a strange and foreign foe. In response they followed the Biblical programming the same way that the ancient Jews did in preparation for war. It is all there, the characterization of your enemy as a devil, the worship of your own chosen God, (democracy in this case) the campaign to get the population scared enough to fight. In times of war, the Old Testament war religions kick in with a vengeance; in times of peace the New Testament concepts are preferred. We choose what to use depending on the circumstances.

*Fearful Myths*

This war programming failed during the Vietnam War. No matter how they tried, the leaders could not convince the people in the USA (especially the educated young people) that they were fighting a foe that threatened the country. They could not get them frightened enough to support the war. This was a very significant failure and is probably partially responsible for the trauma of the returning Vietnam veterans. It is difficult enough to point a gun at another person and kill them knowing that you are doing God's work and protecting your loved ones. It is very much more difficult when the enemy is no real threat and you are not sure why you are fighting the war in the first place.

Killing another person has never been easy and the more educated you get, the harder it becomes. It helps if you can believe that you are in mortal danger and are following the instructions of a very powerful God who will take care of you in the afterlife, but this in itself is not sufficient.

Most people will go out of their way to avoid conflict, but if you get them frightened and angry they will attack almost anything. This is where our social institutions play their part. They all integrate in order to facilitate the development of aggression as this is seen as the essential characteristic for success in our war paradigm.

But this need for aggression limits our freedom. The mental chains needed to force aggression are wrapped around your head at an early age and retained there by constant reinforcement through ritual and social stigma. It is up to you to break them and become free.

You may think that if we no longer fight wars that we wouldn't need the same mechanisms that society developed for war, but let me convince you that this is not the case. Not only are wars fought with guns, but war rules still reign in business, in the Church and in politics.

Freedom is a frightening thing; most of us don't know what we would do with it if we managed to get it and prefer to retain our mental chains. We feel comfortable in our cages and would not risk stepping out even if we could see how to open the door.

If you want to leave this war paradigm, you have to determine where you want to go. It is not sufficient to simply identify some aspects of it that you don't like and try to eliminate them. Unless a comprehensive plan is worked out, we will simply repeat all the mistakes of the past and evolution will be very slow. Our first challenge is to determine what we want to achieve.

But before defining our goals, I want to summarize the arguments and illustrate the patterns which appear when we look at ourselves without the restrictions imposed by the fear-driven socially accepted explanations of our behavior.

# Chapter 5

# Summary

**Where we are coming from**

We are coming out of a war paradigm characterized by:

- Overpowering fear brought on by a hostile environment.

- A war psychology which is reflected in our approach to spirituality, sports, politics, commerce, crime, wealth, just about everything that we do.

- A belief system which characterizes others as enemies unless proved otherwise; this results in

*Summary*

a high level of suspicion of anyone we don't know.

- This creates a social ethic which prescribes:

- Don't question the leaders, they know best and will tell us what we need to know.

- Work hard and expect little for your efforts.

- Low self esteem and the consequential high sensitivity to criticism.

- Control through fear.

- Control those who report to you, copying the style of those above you.

- Goals of accumulating wealth and getting to heaven.

- Pyramid organization structures.

- An expectation to be lead by a remote Godlike figure.

This naturally creates a hostile social environment which perpetuates the paradigm. This war paradigm not only prepares us for war, but also encourages us to see war as the solution to our problems.

## Where we are now

Economic success and a scientific approach to our social prejudices are combining to reduce the level of hostility in the social environment. Many of the rigorous laws of the war paradigm are being questioned and replaced. By projecting this trend into the future we can easily predict subtle changes in society that will have profound effects on our economic environment.

But there is another offsetting trend. As goods become more abundant, the war for resources shifts and becomes a war for markets. The consequences of loosing this war are no different and there is a mad scramble to market goods. This reflects itself in a spiral of cost reduction combined with a confusing abundance of choice. It is not a bed of roses however, as our natural fear of change, combined with increasing uncertainty about the future results in much fear and uncertainty. Meanwhile we live through the transition. Confused by the contradictory messages coming to us we feel powerless to effect the changes we think are necessary. This trap of perceptions forces us to repeat the things that we traditionally do without the conviction that was evident in our forefathers. Carried along by the tide we respond as best we can to the situations presented to us. Without an overall plan, and knowing that individually we are unable to have any effect on the future, we each optimize our own resources while waiting to see what the future will bring.

**Where we are going**

There are two clear paths. One leads to escalating fear as the uncertainty of the world around us causes us to react with hostility, closing doors and shutting off communications. This path leads to war. Perhaps a different kind of war to that we have known in the past, but it will be driven by the same things. Those who don't have the resources necessary to survive will have to take what they want by force. Instead of direct conflict this may take the form of blackmail, kidnapping, terrorist activities, religious enclaves, germ warfare and hundreds of other forms of aggression which no one has thought of yet.

We can see the trend in this direction with the increasing disparity between the rich and the poor – the growth of crime and drugs, the tendency towards religious cults, the increasing hostility between peoples of different beliefs, the alienation of the youth generation. We are becoming more apprehensive about the future. As we move towards oversupply in many industries, the instability that this produces will add fuel to the growing uncertainty, as will the talk of global warming and other environmental disasters.

The other path leads to a much improved quality of life. In many communities, crime is on the decrease and economic activity flourishes. This is

*Summary*

driven by increasing confidence. As long as the level of fear in the community continues to drop, we can expect that the trend away from the war paradigm will continue. Higher levels of education and much better communication will increase our tolerance of others. Growing self-confidence will allow us to give more to the underprivileged in societies, perhaps not directly, but through programs which encourage them to take their own initiatives.

We will be able to do this because we will be confident in the economic theory that shows that a more even distribution of income results in everyone being better off. But to be self-sustaining, this levelling of income has to come through the development of skills, not through direct handouts; hence the need for an increased transfer of knowledge. Following this path we will gradually transition out of the war paradigm into the learning paradigm and remain there as long as we can maintain a low level of fear in the community.

# Chapter 6

# Psycho Fractals

Before moving on to illustrate how the transition to the knowledge paradigm is currently taking place, this chapter summarizes the main patterns outlined so far and shows how the patterns or fractals of history reoccur as the basic fear response is repeated over and over again at different levels in our society. We are all aware of the patterns of history, the fear analysis helps to understand them and use this knowledge to achieve a higher quality of life.

You need to separate yourself from the paradigm of fear before you achieve a position from which the patterns are evident, but this in itself requires a self-confidence that can only be attained by breaking the taboos implanted in your brain when you were very susceptible to fear.

We live in fear of the lord, in fear of the law, disease, crime, natural disaster, accidents... We fear losing our jobs, wives, husbands, and children. We are scared by strangers, threatened by different beliefs and ultimately by death. Fear has shaped our history and in extreme cases has created monsters of us as we reacted to the perceived dangers in a particular era. The Inquisition was driven by fear as was the crucifixion of Jesus. Why did the societies of the time succumb to this group fear which became be all pervading? What is our state of fear at present? Are we are losing confidence in the future? Can we say "our level of fear in society is rising"? In the past, high levels of fear in society has produced some of the most inhumane acts possible by human beings; if we want to avoid repeating these we must understand the effect fear has on each individual in society and how interactions between fearful individuals can elevate the level of fear in a community.

It is with this goal in mind that I introduce you to the idea of a psycho fractal. A fractal is a mathematical term used to describe simple formulae, which create similar patterns when repeated on different scales. Fractals are also referred to as "The patterns of chaos" and many natural things (the shape of a leaf, the patterns of a coastline, the swirl of a Conch shell) seem to follow fractal patterns. The term psycho fractal refers this concept to the rules (or laws) which we repeat on different scales to create the belief systems which define our social paradigm.

The belief, *"There is a God to whom we owe obedience,"* is a simple concept which can be repeated in different contexts. Some of these are:

- *"The boss owns the company and the staff therefore owe him obedience."*

- *"A man's family owes him obedience."*

Because these ideas are closely related to each other, the behavior of the people who act out the roles of boss and family leader follow the behavioral pattern of the God who plays this role for the whole of civilization. Thus, if God is at war with the devil it is also necessary for the boss to be at war with the competition. If the God insists on blind obedience, mysterious messages, and adopts a "you must take no initiative – wait till I tell you what to do" attitude,

*Psycho Fractals*

it can be expected that these "leadership characteristics" will be repeated at each level of the psycho-fractal. It is also true that employees and family members expect their leader to behave as a "God" should. They expect divine guidance, infallibility and adherence to codes of behavior that only gods can achieve.

Unfortunately this expectation is becoming increasingly difficult to maintain, as there is a growing availability of information that illustrates that our leaders, at all levels, are really no different from the rest of us. Our unfulfilled expectations for a "God" to lead us, leaves us angry and frustrated.

In true fractal style the patterns at each level will be varied and no pattern can be exactly compared to another. Today, if the population at large are no longer infatuated with the idea of a "God", they will simply ignore the Church. But, if a family does not behave with the correct deference towards the leader of the household, this person may violently enforce their rules, just as the Church enforced its regime through the Inquisition (1400s) when it felt threatened. This use of force by the Church follows the pattern demonstrated in the

*Understanding Fear*

Bible where the use of force and punishment to ensure that followers obey the leaders is well established.

The stories in the Old Testament Bible describe a cruel, sadistic God tormenting his "children" to ensure that they followed him obediently. When the church leaders were looking for guidance on how to lead their flock they simply repeated this pattern that was again copied by other leaders, as they follow the example of the fractal.

Other Godlike approaches which can be recognized in the related fractals are:

*God is much smarter (by far) than the others and therefore makes all important decisions. The others are stupid and only capable of conveying information or carrying out orders.*

It happens quite often that as soon as we appoint a leader, this person is shrouded in mystery and expected to perform miracles. At the same time the leaders react to this expectation by becoming aloof and frightened and this brings about a change in their behavior as well as a change in the relationship between the leaders and those surrounding them. In many instances, these leaders start to believe that they have more sense than anyone else and experiment with the use of their "awesome power" to intimidate their followers. This behavior should not surprise us, as it is a repeat of the fractal pattern.

When our ancient leaders were looking for a pattern for their organizations they used the same structure that nature selected for man. Every man had a head; therefore every organization has to have a head. Even today we seem to assume that without a leader nothing can be done. If our leaders do not behave with suitable God-like characteristics, then we believe that we may have made a mistake and we try to replace them. As information becomes more easily available, we more quickly lose confidence in our leaders and this process of replacing unsuitable leaders speeds up.

*Understanding Fear*

> *The devil opposes God and causes things to go wrong. Therefore anyone who causes things to go wrong is an agent of the devil and should be punished.*

This is the basis of our legal system of justice. It also contributes to prejudice and to a social behavior that seeks to find "who to blame" instead of "what caused the problem and how can we solve it".

> *We should live in fear of our God and be thankful of any mercy he bestows upon us.*

This would appear to be the expectations of both leaders and followers and both get upset when the idea is challenged, such as when we introduce the idea of a leaderless team in the work place.

When we reflect these behaviors down through the various levels of the psycho fractal and examine management practices and family conflict we see these "God-like" attitudes or expectations displayed in many situations. The Theory X behavior outlined by Douglas McGregor, in his Theory X Theory Y analysis, is derived from the direct application of the psycho fractal taken from Christian theology.

There are many more parallels that can be drawn, but instead of doing this I will examine how and why we created a God in the first place and why we gave him the set of characteristics described in the Old Testament. This will result in a rather brief summary of our history starting in the Middle East around 4,000 BC and touching down at the beginning of the Christian era, the Renaissance and the present.

The population in the Fertile Crescent increased rapidly after the invention of the plow. Increasing skill levels in agriculture, irrigation and animal husbandry resulted in much higher food producing efficiencies and populations grew exponentially. After many generations of exponential expansion, this increasing population eventually resulted in endemic warfare and gradually the "good times" of high economic growth gave way to a fearful existence filled with war and conflict between neighboring tribes.

*Understanding Fear*

The social leaders eventually realized that the fertility gods, which had performed so well during the good years, were no longer of primary importance in this environment and they then created war gods to replace them. These war gods were the epitome of the characteristics needed for survival in a war zone. They were fierce, powerful and cruel leaders who would just as soon kill a dissenter as attack an enemy. These war gods gave essential support to the leaders in the difficult task of converting farmers and traders into warriors and this approach was so successful that it was easy to conclude that it was induced by spiritual beings.

In the social dynamics of the time, if the population did not become warlike, they became slaves. It was this traumatic environment which gave birth to the psycho fractals of the War God which survive in our religion and society today. If you read the books of Exodus with this idea in mind, you will see how difficult it was for the population to abandon a comfortable life and become a warlike tribe and how the "War God" idea was used to achieve this transition. Along with the War God, came a set of stories that helped establish his power and credibility.

*Psycho Fractals*

The Biblical story of Genesis sets the stage for the introduction of the Israeli War God. It credits him with the creation of the world and making it a paradise for man. It blames man's plight (banishment from Eden) on women and the discovery of "good and evil". This is, perhaps, a reference to the population increase and the psycho fractal that divides the world into good and bad. It is important to realize the implications of this idea. Before its introduction, there was no concept of good and bad, but after it became established, there was a strong tendency to blame whatever went wrong on "bad people". You will appreciate that, if everyone is suddenly judging people to be either good or evil, a basis for war is established. This story of Genesis was part of a marketing thrust to establish the Israeli War God as the all-mighty God. It was very successful. This propaganda also establishes the characteristics of the War God whose behavior became the psycho fractal for all people in leadership positions to copy.

The circumstances that brought about the War God religions (endemic warfare) fade from the world from time to time and when this happens society moves away from the war paradigm and starts to develop alternatives. The Romans pacified Palestine around 63 BC and the world in which Jesus lived was probably much more peaceful than previous periods. In response to the mood of the times, Jesus softened the rules of the War God. In so doing he terrified the religious authorities. They were so threatened by this that that they responded with violence. Nevertheless, some of the population seemed to be willing to go along with the change, as long as war did not force them back into the arms of the War Gods. Eventually however the new religion – Christianity – took on many of the characteristics of the older religion from which it was derived and in so doing restored the war paradigm. This probably happened under renewed pressure of war.

The Renaissance arrived about 100 years after the Black Death killed one third to one half the population of Europe (1300 to 1350 AD). I believe that this reduction in population pressure (and eventually war) brought about an environment in which people were no longer overawed by the Christian War God and began to question many things they were being taught by the religious authorities. Once again the religious leaders responded violently to this "work of the devil" by creating the Inquisition and terrorized the population once again. The ideas coming out of the Renaissance lead to the scientific revolution, the Reformation and the industrial revolution. This resulted in a much-increased population. The fractal repeated its pattern and this then inevitably led to war.

At the present time we are once again questioning our basic assumptions and seem to be willing to abandon our dependency on the security blanket provided by religious beliefs. To facilitate this we need a new approach to our social problems, and are now looking for a replacement for the war paradigm psycho fractals. Fortuitously, thanks to modern technology, we have one which applies very well to the present circumstances and which has the simplicity and fractal like behavior that nature seems to love.

When we examine human history one achievement stands out above all others. Fortunes are made and destroyed, empires come and go, but despite this and despite setbacks from time to time, our one crowning achievement over the years has been the accumulation of knowledge. Perhaps we should recognize that this is our destiny. We are here to accumulate knowledge. What we are to do with this knowledge will become apparent as we understand more. How would our society change if our lives and decisions are guided by the psycho fractal "We are here to maximize our knowledge"? As we examine this fractal, at the personal, corporate and state level, some fascinating patterns emerge.

If we are to maximize our own personal knowledge, rather than our personal wealth, we will not depart much from our "accumulate wealth" path until we have been relatively successful in attaining wealth. However, the way we go about accumulating wealth could be quite different as we would naturally try to accumulate wealth and knowledge at the same time and we would try to organize ourselves so that one activity compliments the other.

If we are on the knowledge path we recognize that every interaction with other people is a source of information and because our knowledge – unlike our wealth – is enhanced when it is shared, we are very inclined to share our ideas with others. We therefore try to enhance our communications skills, listen more effectively, communicate in order to understand rather than to enhance our status, and eagerly teach or exchange ideas with our contemporaries. We learn more when we allow our creativity to express itself and we become less averse to going against the mainstream with outlandish suggestions. In short, we become learning individuals.

If we are on the wealth path, we recognize that we have to attain a position of leadership and seek to do this in our own unique way through politics, business, sports, technology etc. But, we are much more status conscious and close-lipped, as high status and exclusive access to information is important. We build an "army" of associates with whom we will cooperate to defeat the "competition" who are the enemy. We use the standard "war paradigm" psycho-fractal to govern our actions and by playing out this fractal our present day society is defined.

Thus the behavior of the "war paradigm" is quite different from that of the "knowledge paradigm". The "knowledge paradigm" adopts a style which is consistent with what many people think of as ideal "Christian" behavior. It is achieved by a simple "maximize your knowledge" fractal, instead of an overbearing set of ancient philosophies and a "do good for others approach" which is hard to sell. It encourages us to be ourselves, be selfish – we want maximum knowledge for ourselves because we enjoy new ideas – but, at the same time, because of the characteristics of information, knowledge and understanding, we do not have to deprive anyone else of what we want. We seem to be genetically designed to follow this fractal as it allows us to do the things we like to do!

At a corporate level the "knowledge paradigm" creates "learning organizations" – information flows freely, decision-making is done at the lowest possible organizational level, bosses become obsolete. These ideas are developed and expanded in some of the more recent corporate literature such as "Business Without Bosses" by Charles C. Manz... The "Learning Organization" by Bob Garratt... "The Fifth Discipline" by Peter M. Senge... "The Seven Habits of Highly Effective People" by Stephen R. Covey. I will not expand on them here. This sector seems well advanced in following the "knowledge is my goal" psycho fractal. But it is fascinating to recognize another pattern.

The war religions probably evolved long after man had converted his tribe to a war machine and the religious characters were made to "follow the pattern" of leadership characteristics that were essential for success in war, thus giving support to the war effort. In the same way the techniques being evolved "at the front" today i.e. in our business battles, is finding its way into our social structure. There is no doubt that "business" is the most evolved entity in this reshaping of society to a knowledge paradigm, and I am suggesting that the rest of society will follow.

At a governmental level, the "maximize knowledge" psycho fractal becomes a governmental goal to maximize the knowledge base of society. Their first step is to gradually reduce the restrictions on information flow. Here lies a fundamental difference between the war paradigm and the learning paradigm. The war approach assumes that the leaders are smart and knowledgeable and followers are stupid and have to be told and sometimes forced to behave in a correct manner. This assumption helps define the shape of society in way that leads to conflict – it is slowly being challenged as we see in Tunisia and Egypt. On the other hand the "learning" psycho fractal encourages and facilitates "good guys" (it assumes that people are basically good) to flourish. This requires an open transparent economy with a minimum of regulations.

If we could find a way through the mayhem that might take place with the freeing up of information in society, we may be able to tackle some of our major problems. Could drug traders exist in a society in which everyone knows who they are? Yes – probably as well as South Africa survived with apartheid. The criminal element in our society revel in the secrecy provided by our laws, but on the other side of the information deluge we might not need punishment to bring these people into line. A society keyed on knowledge as the prime goal will behave differently and may apply social pressure to minimize antisocial behavior.

The process of questioning our basic beliefs is well underway. If we can stay away from warfare for long enough, this process may result in a totally different society. Many people are becoming optimistic, while others see escalating personal conflict (child and wife battering, etc.) along with the increasing polarization over issues such as abortion, as evidence of the emotional build up that precedes heightened conflict.

We all know that a family may quarrel between themselves, but unite when there is an external threat. The reverse is also true. One characteristic of our social "war paradigm" is the tendency for internal conflict to replace external conflict when the external conflict disappears. This is evident in the break-up of the USSR and in the impasse between the US president and congress over bringing government spending into line. The need to do this is a reflection of financial and economic fears.

The world went into a recession in the 1930's. Prior to that recession the stock market was booming, there was over production of goods and there was a feeling that government spending should be reduced – they had been spending at an exceptional rate. This fear of overspending is healthy – but if it is not controlled it leads to violent economic swings. No one wants to be in debt when confidence is low, but economists will argue that balanced budget =

low confidence = recession. Perhaps, as this fractal plays itself out, the thing that follows recession is war, as nations get scared of their neighbors. Although present conditions are very similar, we believe that we largely have our economies under control. But we cannot control human beings with mechanistic things. We are losing our confidence in the future and very low interest rates can only go so far to influence this. A new spiritual injection is needed. Will this come from the traditional war or from a "maximize knowledge" psycho fractal?

You may have noticed that this approach does not seek to blame anyone for the past. Instead it is clearly focused on what we have to do to increase our knowledge base. This shift in emphasis from "blame" to "seeking knowledge" is one of the significant characteristics of the new paradigm. Can you imagine what would happen to our society if this shift became widespread?

When the ancients realized that they needed a new approach to cope with the increasingly warlike nature of their society they found that changing their religion had a big impact on the process. We must do a similar thing. I am suggesting that what we have to do is to play out the fractal "maximize knowledge" on all possible scales, including the spiritual; but before outlining my ideas in that area let me illustrate how the transition to the knowledge paradigm is presently affecting us.

# Chapter 7

# Goals

Our present goals are inextricably entwined with the beliefs of the war paradigm. Programmed to win wars, we find ingenious ways to force everything we do into a war. In this war paradigm the goal is to win. To leave this paradigm different goals must be established.

By rejecting the idea that Western religions were handed down to man by God, we are making fundamental shifts to our social organization. There is a symbiotic relationship between our spiritual and social inventions with one copying the other in form, if not content. The goal of everlasting happiness in heaven or the consequences of everlasting pain in hell is mirrored in our social environment. It helps to motivate the constant pursuit of material wealth, the heaven on earth, to match the promise of the spiritual concept. These two goals are interrelated and if one disappears, the other will go as well.

While it is easy to find fault with many aspects of our social environment, it is at the same time very difficult to prescribe something different. This difficulty also applies to our traditional goals – easy to criticize, hard to replace. Once we aim for wealth, we are forced to live in a paradigm which induces conflict. Wealth cannot be shared. You either have it or someone else has it. If you consume it or give it away you no longer have it. But wealth cannot be our primary goal it can only be a means to an end. In this environment, the fundamental question: "What is our ultimate goal?" is not addressed.

Let me suggest that, instead of seeking wealth, our prime goal be the accumulation and application of knowledge. *This makes learning our fundamental reason for living.* This is a simple and profound statement and is in tune with spiritual development ideas from many cultures. We must accumulate knowledge while accepting that as we learn more, we will gradually be able to make better sense of this role.

Think of a little child who asks the question; "What will I be when I grow up?" Can you explain it? Chances are your best advice to the child is to try their best at all they do and gradually the answers will appear. The same situation applies to the whole human race. What we need to do is to press on with our development as best we can knowing that our role will gradually become clearer as we accumulate more and more knowledge. Many cultures encourage the quest for enlightenment and expect that the seeker will gradually understand more as he experiences life. This experience, along with the guidance of the master, results in a rewarding life.

This is what I call the learning paradigm. Essentially we are here to learn. This is the reason for our existence; this is what makes us happy; this is our prime goal. But to accept this as a wonderful solution, you first have to appreciate that our Western culture can be adapted to this goal with little fundamental change to our way of life. Learning is instinctive and fun. We can migrate from being servants of our almighty God to seekers of knowledge while enjoying the process and being much more productive in our jobs.

*Goals*

No one has to tell children that they should learn. It comes naturally and they start as soon as they can. Some even argue that this process starts before birth. Children are inquisitive and learn at a fantastic rate up to the point when they become afraid. Then the learning slows down, at least in some directions. After a child learns that something is dangerous, they avoid it and the learning process stops advancing in that direction.

Fear blocks learning and if you want to learn about something you first have to overcome or find a way around the fear. In June 1633, Galileo was condemned by the Pope to life imprisonment for claiming that the Earth was not at the center of the universe. His theories threatened the Church, as they appeared to oppose what the Church was preaching at the time. The Church responded, as we all do when sufficiently threatened, with violence. This is my favorite example, but there are an abundance of others, where social pressures are brought to bear on people making startling advances on the edge of science. Their ideas pose a threat and society acts to minimize the perceived danger. As a result information that can lead to an improved quality of life is not forthcoming. This process repeats itself over and over again.

Cloning is a more recent threat. We can envisage horrible people taking advantage of us through cloning. It is a threat to our way of life and we don't know how to handle it so we react with emotional violence and in so doing follow the pattern of the war paradigm. There are many reasons that could be advanced for objecting to cloning, but I would bet that very, very few people would say "This thing scares me, and I don't want you to do it until I am comfortable with it." But this would be close to the truth.

As we enter the information age, we need to adopt a philosophy that manages fear and facilitates learning. The goal to maximize learning does this.

Our competitive society is evolving to the stage where we recognize that information, and the knowledge that can be distilled from it, is the key to success. Businessmen understand that increasing the rate at which a company can absorb and apply knowledge leads to a competitive advantage. Educators know that, in order for children to learn at a faster rate they have to take responsibility for their own learning. Instead of going to school and being tough, they have to go to school to gather information that they are interested in. The same transfer of responsibility is being sought in the business world where employers are asking employees to take more responsibility. In our homes we are recognizing that we need to ensure that our children have confidence in themselves so that they feel free to communicate with us and have the ability to make their own decisions without being unduly influenced by peer pressure.

This trend away from hierarchical dominance is well established and heralds a fundamental change in our social organization that is closely related to the shift in emphasis from wealth to learning. But there are other implications in this change in goals. We are shifting from goals which are related to status to those which are related to flows.

Human beings make extensive use of feedback control. If we get too hot, a control system regulates our body functions to return us to the optimum temperature. If too much light is arriving at our eyes, a control system closes the pupils to reduce this to an acceptable level. There are many others, our bodies are filled with them. These control systems are excellent at ensuring that a dynamic system achieves a desired status. This goal is set and the system controls itself through measuring the output and comparing it to the desired set point. An air-conditioning system is another good example. The temperature is set on the thermostat and the system controls itself to achieve the set temperature.

At a more spiritual level, we can appreciate that we are all programmed to reach a goal. This goal is happiness and we do what we can to be happy. We tend to think that riches bring happiness so we seek wealth. But closer examination reveals that this idea cannot stand up to rigorous examination. Wealth does not necessarily lead to happiness. We need to apply the self-knowledge gained from the fear analysis to come up with a better understanding of what makes us happy.

In the war paradigm, the only acceptable way to be happy is to follow the lord's (boss's, father's, politician's) instructions – work hard and live the simple life; any other behavior is suspect. The war paradigm assumes that we are intrinsically bad and will be tempted to do evil. The low self esteem of that paradigm has a strong influence and it is assumed that we are so weak that if we let go of the rigid controls imposed by the Protestant ethic that we immediately loose the battle against evil temptations. The fear of being easily tempted results in our building a protective mechanism that has a major impact on our behavior. When we move away from this fear, we can examine our behavior with less emotion and more rationalism and see the parallels between how our society operates and how other physical systems operate. Let me draw some parallels to systems theory.

In developing the theory on which the feedback control systems are based, engineers came up with the idea of two classes of variables that were important. One related to flow. Fluids, gasses, heat and electric currents flow through circuits or systems and can be measured to determine the rate of flow. The other variable is sometimes called an across variable as it measures the voltage, pressure and temperature change that takes place when the flow passes through an element of the circuit. Energy is a function of the combination of these two variables.

*Understanding Fear*

Let me draw a parallel and describe happiness as the product of a flow variable and an across variable so that happiness depends on both the action that is taking place and the change in status which results from that action. Those who are familiar with physical systems will immediately realize that happiness is defended in the same way as energy. In abbreviated terms, Happiness = Energy. To spell it out, happiness is dependent on the action we take to achieve a desired status multiplied by the resultant status change. The idea is very simple. To be happy we have to be active. This activity is the flow. We must also know what we hoped to achieve by this action and when our action produces the expected result we are happy.

Think of a young child learning to walk. She crawls over to a chair and by the combined action of hands and feet she gets into a standing position for the first time. She flashes a smile and chuckles. Energy seems to emanate from her. She is very happy, but this fades quickly and she is soon concentrating on taking her first step. We all repeat this process daily as we face various challenges. If we are successful, if we take action and achieve our desired result, we are happy. If we don't take action, or if our actions don't move us towards our desired goal, we are unhappy.

It's important to understand what produces happiness, because it is our ultimate goal. Just as we understand that the happiness that results from a full stomach is our reward for having been successful hunters, we must also understand that the happiness that we get from more intellectual success is also a genetically programmed result. We may not know why this particular action makes us happy, but we know it is there and we should follow it.

Many will argue that if we simply pursue happiness, we will allow the society to degenerate into uncivilized behavior. My counter to this argument is that uncivilized behavior is typical of frightened people. As we move away from the war paradigm and understand the effects of fear, we will be able to control our environments to reduce the level of fear and this will induce a positive behavioral change. It has to be a gradual process. If the social restraints are suddenly removed, the abrupt change will frighten us and we will revert to antisocial behavior. On the other hand if self confidence is built up slowly, there comes a point where we are confident to stand on our own in the spiritual world, just as the little child stands on their own when learning to walk.

In our war paradigm we wish and strive for status because we think that this will make us happy. What other people think of us is important. This drives us to pay attention to the way we look, how we dress, the way we behave. It is all geared to impress others. A vague feeling that more money will put is in a better position drives us to work. Few understand that *action in the right direction is the essential component that produces happiness*. Even fewer question the traditional goals of society and examine these to see if they make sense.

We see pictures of people on TV acting out the role of being happy – the quiz show winner, the hero who has beaten the villain, the scientist with the big discovery, the athlete winning the big race, the winning football team. We all would like to be there, to enjoy this orgasm of achievement. But this is only the orgasm; the real enjoyment is the act, the process of getting there. This is why the Protestant ethic is doomed. It worked while people could believe that by slaving away they were working towards everlasting happiness, but this idea is lost. Servitude is out. It is no longer an acceptable component in the relationship to the local boss and will eventually work its way out of the approach to the spiritual boss.

Most people who end up being very good at something enjoy the process of getting there. The star athlete enjoys running, he does not do it simply to get the prize; he does it because he enjoys the process of training and interfacing with coaches and the crowds, and he enjoys the recognition. He enjoys the whole process, not just the winning moment. Businessmen like making profits, not because they need the money, but because they like the process. Many of the most successful businessmen I know will never have the opportunity to enjoy their wealth by spending it. They invest it and enjoy the challenge this poses. But few will accept that this is enjoyable. They are so absorbed with the ideas of the Christian ethic that they think that they are very uncomfortable. They think that they are "working hard" and are not getting sufficient social recognition for their efforts.

*Understanding Fear*

We need to understand that we are enjoying ourselves when we are "working hard" and toss aside the idea that we are working because this is essential for our survival. That somehow, because we work hard society owes us something (over and above our salary) for the contribution we have made. This is another of the ideas that are related to servitude which needs to be removed from our psyche.

One of the characteristics of a system which is controlled by a feedback mechanism is its consistency of purpose. Nothing short of disaster can stop the controls from working and directing the system along specific lines. When you drive a car, you get to your destination – roadblocks, traffic jams, wrong turnings, diversions or anything else cannot prevent you from getting to your destination. If you are determined to get there you will. This characteristic is typical of feedback control systems and when we see this characteristic in nature, we can anticipate that there is some control mechanism at work.

I invite you to examine the history of the human race with this in mind. Most histories deal with wars as important events, but ignore these for a minute. Look at the march of human development.

*Goals*

Where learning has been encouraged and supported, the societies have been very successful. From time to time this progress is halted or reversed, but eventually it reestablishes itself. The irrefutable conclusion is that we are programmed to increase knowledge. It would appear that we have been on a course of increasing our knowledge since prehistoric times. Diversions happen, but these do not change our direction, they simply slow us down a bit. Whenever we get past the diversion we continue our path to increased knowledge. We are programmed with a control mechanism that produces this need to know. When we are on track we are happy, when we get diverted we are unhappy. The whole war paradigm has been a diversion.

Our status goals work as long as they make us learn while demonstrating some progress towards the goal we have set, but fundamentally it is the learning, the experiences, that create the happiness. We should recognize that we don't have to live a life of hardship in order to make progress; we can enjoy our experiences and still achieve our goal of learning.

*Understanding Fear*

This apparently anticlimactic conclusion is in fact a tremendous discovery. It links to the Eastern religions which emphasize flow with the Western philosophies which emphasize status and it relates both to physical systems which engineers have studied in great detail. When concepts come together like this, it gives you the feeling that you are on the right track even if the results are not what you expected. We are all attuned to conceptualize goals as milestones along the path. We want to own a car, or become a manager, or a bus driver. We see our progress in achieving these milestones and we expect that the road between these points will be rough and difficult. To now say that we should not only achieve the milestones along the way but also enjoy the trip, is quite a departure from our expectations. To also say that the milestones should not be the externally glamorous ones that we have been taught to aim for, but that they should be defined in terms of our own self-development is another departure from expectations.

But it all ties together. Nature shows us a system with two fundamentally different types of variables and we have learnt what happens when

*Goals*

these are combined. We have to initiate the process of getting rid of the very limiting ideas handed to us as gospel truths and reexamine our mental chains. They are figments of our imagination. We have to open our own internal doors and windows and look at the things that we have been frightened to look at before. If anyone else does it for us we easily accept the role of a follower. But this traps us in a hierarchical paradigm and we continue to play the role of the follower. Instead of this each of us has to take the lead down our own individual path to self-development.

It will take a lot of courage to climb out from under the ancient beliefs which shield us from knowledge and which have evolved into our social genetic code from more desperate times, but an eventful road to freedom awaits those who try.

Nature gives another good example that we can use to understand the process. When a child is born there is a separation from the mother. There is trauma and fear, but well nurtured, the child grows independent and eventually takes its own path. We must all individually follow this pattern, both physically and spiritually, and instead of following the instructions of our gods we must make use of our natural abilities to guide our own path. As illustrated in the painting on the roof of the Sistine Chapel in Rome, we have to let go of God. He has done his job; we now have to move on under the force of our own will, set our own goals. I invite you to accept that increasing knowledge is the best way to achieve this. Each of us must have the prime goal to become a learning individual.

To exit the war paradigm, we must have a direction, a goal, but this in itself is not sufficient and we must also be able to manage fear, as fear blocks learning. This is where our history can help. Many techniques for managing fear are illustrated in our history books, and like most things, there are advantages and disadvantages associated with each one. We have the fascinating task of developing a new approach to fear by setting new goals and experimenting with new techniques. Each attempt will teach us something new. This is all we need.

# Chapter 8

# War Paradigm to Learning Paradigm

This transition has been in progress for a long time. We are now getting to the exciting stage, the point at which we come over the brow of the hill and see the Promised Land. It does not fit with our expectations, but we also recognize that we want to be surprised. If this new paradigm had fit our expectations we would have been disappointed.

The Christian movement was a valiant attempt to get away from the war paradigm. Peace, tolerance and understanding were featured along with a drift away from the strict laws and rituals of the Jewish religion. But it did not achieve separation. The character of the father, the old War God, still dominated what evolved to become Christianity and instead of breaking away from fear and establishing the self confidence of their flock, the movement got drawn back into the paradigm of fear, and, instead of celebrating a new understanding of human nature it ended up reinforcing the guilt of the fall with the guilt of the crucifixion. This increased the climate of fear rather than reducing or managing it.

The Renaissance was another attempt to break the grip of fear and control that the Church maintained. But this initiative threatened the Church and it reacted with the hysteria of a terrified person. Just as the Jewish authorities reacted to the threatening teachings of Jesus with violence, the Roman Catholic Church attacked the ideas of the Renaissance. The Church saw the devil gaining ground and this sent them into a panic. They responded by setting up of the Inquisition to eliminate evil people with strange ideas from the face of the earth. The hysteria that this created along with the tortures, forced confessions and deaths is part of the historical record and signals the extent of the terror that the was felt at the time.

Both of these attempts to break the mental chains and allow people the freedom of self-determination failed at the time, but they contributed considerably to the progress of our civilization. The present movement in this direction got going in the 1950's with Douglas McGregor and Abraham Maslow both making major contributions to the theories on motivation which were then being studied. This lead to the ideas generated by Edwards Demming that became known as Total Quality Management. The continued evolution of these ideas leads to the learning organization. Along the way several old ideas had to be updated, but the underlying war philosophy still holds the fort.

These tentative explorations along a different path need a philosophy to replace the old war paradigm philosophy, link the trends together, explain the apparent contradictions and give direction. The learning paradigm can provide this. Many of the anomalies that we see in our society are explained by this concept that also helps to reduce the trauma of the transition. You need to have faith in the human race, we are very intelligent people and once we learn how to recognize and manage our fear a new world awaits us.

The learning organization is a concept driven by the learning paradigm. It seeks to graduate the corporation from being a beast of burden or a slave to its shareholders and give it a separate status as a free person. This is a significant step and will happen. It is predicted by the fractal pattern and follows the trend best symbolized by the emancipation of slavery. Just as the owners of slaves saw emancipation as a very threatening thing and resisted it, we can expect that corporate shareholders will also resist the movement to free corporations from their control, but it is already happening.

Unless shareholders have direct involvement in a business, they can exercise very limited control and are placed in the position of being an investor rather than an owner. In effect their position as an owner has already been eroded. But in the corporate world the statement "The profits belong to the shareholders" is given divine status. When I question it, I get blank faces, and I gather that the question has not been understood. So let me ask it here and advance my reasoning for doing so.

Why do we believe that corporate profits belong to the shareholders? The quick answer is that they are defined in law as owners of the corporation –

corporations are the slaves of the shareholders. However they are slaves with a great deal of freedom, so the slavery model does not work. Perhaps a better model is that of an army. One of the historical roots of the modern corporation is in being a supplier or contractor to armies. But like large armies in developing states, they have an independent base of power. I am thinking of the army in Egypt and its recent role as a power broker. There is an element of corporate behavior that mimics this role. But while each of these models has some relevance, neither does a good job of defining the role of the corporation in modern society so I will use elements of the behavior of each to help develop a workable image of the large corporation.

Suppose we think of them as slaves and then give them freedom. The first response would be large executive salaries and wild actions as the yolk of being burdened by years of servitude is released. During this period the CEO's try to emulate the traditional image of being in control while there is still the semblance of control by the shareholders and the executives are still driven to maximize the wealth of the shareholders. Like armies they maintain strict hierarchical structures and go forth to conquer their enemies. This trend continues for some time, but this period is a transition and comes to an end.

Sooner or later the next stage starts where these executives realize that they really don't have to maintain the value of the shares unless they need to go to that market for further investment. In many cases these corporations will be cash rich, the opportunities for new investment are limited and so they will not have to go to the market for cash in the foreseeable future. Why then maintain the share price, why try to maximize the price of the corporation's shares if you don't need to sell any? The threat of a hostile takeover maintains traditional behavior as well as share options and incentive schemes, but the writing is on the wall, change is at hand. In the wider community the problem is one of oversupply, underemployment and an ever-increasing division between rich and poor. As conditions change, an image that includes social and environmental responsibility becomes marketable and corporate advertising leaps to the opportunity. These advertisements affect the staff in the corporation as well as their customers and the seeds of change have an opportunity to grow. Sooner or later, while examining the opportunities for new markets, the vast potential offered by billions of poor people become more enticing; growth opportunities can be generated if the purchasing power of these people is increased. But exploiting these markets requires answering a difficult question; how do you get money into the hands of poor people so that they can buy your goods?

As life goes on the shareholder is conceptually replaced with the stakeholder, and then gradually replaced in practice. This occurs because executives realize that the long established trend in the nature of work, from being simple, manual tasks to being complicated highly skilled value added contributions, is also forcing the learning paradigm closer and closer. It is no longer possible to control with fear, or give simple clearly understood instructions for the operation of the business. Employees are no longer submissive and gain a better understanding of their worth to the corporation. The "We the worker – They the management" division can no longer be sustained as the intimate contact needed between these groups, along with the need to invest heavily in training, breaks down this long established traditional barrier.

But the servitude does not leave easily as there is nothing to replace it. Gradually, however, the concepts of the learning paradigm take over and a different approach to corporate governance takes hold. There is a greater willingness to share the economic added value of the corporation with the employees, who are now considered stakeholders in the business, becoming part of the team. Eventually the idea of servitude is replaced with self-determination and the vision and mission statements of the corporation incorporate the concept of continual learning. This change is gradual and as the ideas change, organizational habits and structures change as well.

One of the things which is ripe for change is the organizational structure which has maintained its pyramid shape since invented by the Egyptians. They were so impressed with it that they gave it divine status. It is interesting to note that when computers were first developed they were designed in accordance with this structure. Very soon however the bureaucracy of this organization proved to be too cumbersome and instead of main frames and dumb terminals we began to see file servers, networks and smart workstations. Perhaps the revolution that is currently going on in Egypt can be seen as a similar transition.

In a computer network no one particular machine is in charge. The rules for the transfer of information are very precise. Each entity plays its individual part as an independent operator. This structure mirrors that of the broader private sector where individual companies interface with each other, with no one company being in charge. A similar change is also taking place in the organizational structure within businesses where teams are being used to replace the boss and servant concept. If this structure evolves similarly to that in the computer world, we can expect that individuals will become more responsible for the decision making while calling on the services of specialized resource personnel (the equivalent of file servers) in specific areas of expertise.

In this migration away from status rich structures, bosses evolve to become coaches who advise and consul, while the people in the ranks are automatically elevated as the structures become flatter. They are now expected to make more and more decisions in the course of their work instead of waiting for decisions to arrive from above. This transition heralds the arrival of the knowledge paradigm because it requires a much enhanced level of training and a very much wider distribution of information.

Instead of being hoarded by the boss, information is gradually being shared in these organizations, but this also requires a closer working relationship between the boss and the rest of the organization as now a higher level of trust is required and this can only be established where there is general agreement on the sharing of rewards for the work effort and acceptance of the other person as a part of the team. This is not an easy transition and is being resisted as in most cases neither the bosses nor the subordinates are entirely happy with their new roles.

The coordination of the whole organization which used to take place in the bosses head now has to be achieved throughout a host of mini bosses and to achieve this corporate mission statement, goals and operational guidelines become much more important. This is all happening at a time when traditional work methods are constantly being reviewed as the computer technology now available to the workforce requires different methods of working.

The idea of a knowledge worker is being discussed along with the concept of teamwork, but these changes are not easily accepted and employees at all levels exhibit withdrawal, aggression, mental violence or apathy, all indicators of a high level of fear. To make matters worse, the progressive changes taking place in the workplace are not mirrored in the rest of society where the heightened level of fear at work affects social behavior and society reacts to this by moving to the right and becoming more dependent on charismatic leaders who wave flags and whip up enthusiasm for war; be it the war about the environment, the one for social security, abortion, gay rights, warlords in Somalia, drug barons, terrorism etc. This characteristic human reaction is probably similar in many respects to the social responses which accompanied many other changes which are recorded in history.

Another social phenomena associated with this stress is the arrival of the Sports God and the associated tribal identity that is now provided by brand names in the fashion industry. The worship of these gods takes place while watching television or

*Understanding Fear*

while wearing the shoes, hats or clothing endorsed by these superhuman beings. The same pattern is repeated at a different level. The tendency to form gangs and go to war that can be seen in the inner cities is also a response to the fear of unknown change. The young people find themselves unable to determine what they can do to manage their level of fear and form gangs and bad together in a desperate attempt to defend themselves from an unseen enemy.

Despite these negative trends, much more effort is being devoted to training. This brings self-confidence and the ability to accept new ideas more easily. But even though the effort is being made, progress is extremely slow as what is being taught undermines the war paradigm and the confusion that results when the theory does not fit the practice make these new ideas very difficult to understand and accept. As a result a compromise position, such as that worked out between the Old and New Testaments appears to be in the making while the transition to a new paradigm waits on an underlying philosophy to make it more understandable and acceptable.

*War Paradigm to Learning Paradigm*

The stress of the transition is also showing up in law enforcement, where the moral will to inflict the death penalty, so long supported by our religious training, is slipping and in many countries this penalty is either being abolished or is being made so legally difficult that the condemned person is held on death row for many years. Without the moral will to kill someone who has killed, and with no alternative suggesting itself, this process is bogged down and awaits new thinking.

One of the principal flaws in the legal process is the idea that you can correct a mistake (or crime) that has already happened and compensate the aggrieved party. While this appears to work when the damages can be related to dollars, the flaw of logic is very apparent when we set it against an extreme condition such as murder where it becomes immediately apparent that the victim cannot be compensated. This quandary illustrates that we are attempting to both compensate and punish with the legal process.

While the compensation portion seems to have a reasonable basis, the punishment portion needs a God-like almighty force of conviction for it to continue. This is fading and will continue to fade as the war paradigm closes. It eventually will be replaced with fear management. Recognizing that people respond to their environments, we will work to remove those things from the environment that force people into crime. The implementation of such corrective measures will eventually reduce the stream of people arriving at the courts; in the interim we will continue to have to support the punishment deterrent.

The transition is also apparent in other spheres of social activity such as where the overburdening fear of women and sex, propagated by the Christian myths are having less influence on the population as a whole. Celibacy is losing its appeal to the clergy, women are being considered for the priesthood, premarital sex is the norm, nudity is not a sin on certain beaches, women are being recognized as the intellectual equals of men, single parent families are more prevalent, family planning is becoming the norm, same sex couples are becoming more accepted.... the trend is evident. Each step along the way is a fight with those elements in society that retain the taboos of the Christian beliefs, and battles are continually being fought, with violence in some areas such as abortion and gay rights.

These taboos, like the others, were set up in order for the population to be successful in fighting wars, and have continued to exist long after the need for them has diminished. Instead of taboos to support the Biblical *"Go forth and populate the world"* we need a rational approach to population control and it is interesting to note the growing realization that the best method of controlling population is education; another plug for the knowledge paradigm.

We seem to have arrived at the stage in our development where rationality can be used to manage our destiny and an underlying philosophy for this rationality would help considerably in aiding our understanding of the transition that is taking place. I don't think we should try to stop or slow down what is happening; that would be futile. Instead we should apply our rationality to the process and manage it as best we can. Apart from guiding us in the application of our resources, this new philosophy is essential to detoxify the old taboos of the war paradigm that are mainly propagated through our religions.

When the ancient world was dissolving into warfare it took a very long time for an operating philosophy to evolve. According to my limited research, evidence of warfare goes back to 10,000 BC while the emergence of the most highly evolved war gods (The Christian and Muslim Gods) only appeared after 1,000BC. At the time the individual tribes were powerless to stop the development of war and their best chance of survival was to develop fighting skills rather than trying to stop the process. Similarly today we are facing a situation where we can't stop the evolution of our civilization and have to develop the skills needed to exist in this new environment.

But the pace of social evolution is increasing rapidly and we need to ensure that a new philosophy emerges quickly, before the prejudices inherited from the past start the cycle of war all over again. Evidence of the rapid change can be gleaned from watching the progress of this transition on a global basis as the same forces act in many different areas of endeavor.

To summarize the trends:

| From: **Prejudice is good** | To: **Prejudice is bad** |
|---|---|
| it supports the tribe, locks out strangers, increases security, helps guarantee a future that we can accept. Strangers in our midst threaten us and make us very uncomfortable. We need to remove them to better ensure survival of the tribe. | on the basis of race creed and culture, but OK between businesses, sports teams, political parties, different religions... |

**Comment:** As long as we continue to fight wars, prejudice will be with us. As the armies change into sports teams, the nature of the prejudice changes. Just as we are working diligently to destroy the prejudices developed in the past, we are carefully creating prejudices to carry with us into the future. But these are less severe. We can more easily switch sides and be welcomed by the opposition. As the trend continues and we recognize that there are alternatives to war. I expect that the need for prejudice will diminish to the stage where it is no longer a social issue.

*Understanding Fear*

| From: **Fear is essential** | To: **Fear must be managed** |
|---|---|
| Fear of God helps to ensure that we don't stray into the devil's path. Fear of our parents, school teachers and priests forces us to be good. Fear of the consequences, keeps us away from crime. Fear of our boss makes us work hard. Instilling fear in children and employees helps them to be good. Respect for authority is essential, this is achieved by fear. | High levels of fear produce violence and result in stress, sickness, loss of productivity, high medical costs. It blocks good communication and decision-making. We do however need a manageable level of fear in our life – it is not the enemy, it is a part of us and we need to understand it and manage it. |

**Comment:** People are rebelling against a high fear regime and are demanding a better quality of life. Fear only motivates when the task is simple and can be learnt easily. It de-motivates where there are complicated decisions to be made and many points of view have to be considered. As the world becomes more complicated, its usefulness will diminish and alternative ways of motivation will be developed.

*War Paradigm to Learning Paradigm*

| From: **Follow the leader** | To: **Self determination** |
|---|---|
| We are stupid, despicable creatures and unable to make it on our own. We need to join a tribe for support, to be nurtured and led. In return we work hard to support the tribe, follow its dictates and don't question its beliefs. | We are smart intelligent creatures. We associate freely with those we like. We are capable of being independent and make our own decisions. We question everything and seek to understand rather than believe. |

**Comment:** This is a natural trend in an environment of reducing fear. The reverse happens when the level of fear increases. Our politicians seek to heighten the level of fear of the enemy during election campaigns and thus increase support for the tribe. They are using a well established fear response, but when this is understood it becomes much less effective and will result in different political strategies being adopted. Understanding this will help us get beyond it.

| **From:** **Motivation through threat and reward** | **To:** **Motivation through goal achievement, curiosity and competition** |
|---|---|
| To get someone to do something, you either have to threaten them with dire consequences if it is not done, or reward them for doing it. In most cases both threat and reward are offered. | Goals are expressed as flows rather than milestones (I want to feel successful, rather than I want to make a million dollars). Curiosity and innovation are encouraged. Competition is a relay race rather than a fight. |

**Comment:** The academic community sits on the edge of the war paradigm. Sometimes it gets drawn into it, lured by the glitter of the big bucks. The rest of the community moves away from war as the environment becomes less hostile. We respond to the reduced threat by becoming more civilized. Death penalties and other forms of corporal punishment are seen as inhuman, employees respond better to inducement rather than threat. Children revolt and leave homes where fear is used as the prime motivator. We pose more questions of those in authority. All these trends are in response to the changing environment.

*War Paradigm to Learning Paradigm*

| From: **Competition = Boxing match** | To: **Competition = Track and Field** |
|---|---|
| Direct attack of the opposition is the main feature. | Interference with competitors is taboo. |

**Comment:** We have a natural tendency to want to be better than those around us. This exists even when the environment is not threatening. In some cases, where self-confidence is low, the risk of losing becomes a threat in itself and this drives unsocial behavior.

| From: **Pyramid organizations** | To: **Network organizations** |
|---|---|
| The boss is in charge and is in complete control. The followers take orders and support the power structure. Information is controlled. | Each individual pursues their own goals and uses their initiative to best achieve them while co-ordinating their activity with others in the same organization or community. Information flows with little restriction. |

**Comment:** First invented to fight wars, the pyramid structure permeates all organizations as they are all conceptually fighting wars, but they are becoming inefficient as the level of complexity of the organizations increases and networks perform better.

*War Paradigm to Learning Paradigm*

| **From:** <br> **Goal is survival** | **To:** <br> **Goal is to learn** |
|---|---|
| This leads to differentiation and separation and a *we versus they* approach. Religious groups and ethnic groups openly demonstrate this survival modus operandi, which includes a set of beliefs and rituals which prop-agate the separation and results in friction between groups. | Gaining knowledge is seen as a fun occupation that benefits the individual as well as the community. Integration follows, based on respect for the knowledge that others bring with them. The redirection of our energy away from fighting results in a quantum leap in the quality of life. |

**Comment:** This trend is apparent in the corporate world where large companies are merging. The mergers allow closer cooperation between former competitors and allow more energy to be directed to research and development. There is also a trend for these large organizations to be organized in less hierarchical structures, some are experimenting with network structures.

| From: | To: |
|---|---|
| **Protection of the child within** | **Expose the child so it can grow** |
| Our natural reaction to threat is to build a wall around the vulnerable child within us. Behind this wall the child remains a child and never gets beyond the wall. | Feel the fear; see it as signal that all is not well. Understand the threat; strengthen the child within to deal with the threat. |

**Comment:** When the world is a fearsome place with enemies all around, a good strategy is to build walls, just as the Europeans in the Middle Ages built castles to protect themselves. When the world becomes friendlier a more open strategy is appropriate. Hence we see large trade groupings being formed. We are essentially saying that we can risk more exposure. The American culture has been successful because it encourages its children to believe that there is nothing that they cannot achieve. Other cultures place more emphasis on protecting their children by maintaining taboos that ensure that they do not stray into dangerous areas.

| From: | To: |
|---|---|
| **Emphasis on youth** | **Emphasis on the wisdom which comes with experience** |
| Our present culture emphasizes youth because this is the traditional warrior. We anticipate that young warriors, led by a successful older warrior will win the battles that we face. Old people are useless as they no longer have the drive to fight. They are a burden that society has to deal with. | Some people rise above the battering they get as a normal participant in the act of living. These people are valued for their wise council. As more people understand themselves better and learn more through their exposure to life, they will accumulate wisdom that will become very valuable to society. |

**Comment:** In the war paradigm the older leaders tend to be great warriors. The more enlightened older people have decided that war is not worthwhile and have diverted their attention elsewhere. As we move out of the war paradigm, these more enlightened people will be brought into the mainstream of social development.

| From: **Hierarchical approach to spirituality** | To: **Networking approach to spirituality** |
|---|---|
| We are slaves to the spirits who created us. We owe these masters our allegiances and are indebted to them because we screwed up their instructions. As a result we are being punished. | This involves a different relationship with the spiritual world. We no longer think of spirits as our masters, instead they become our associates and we interface with them to maximize knowledge. |

**Comment:** This will be a very difficult change for many who have consoled themselves with the idea that they are doing God's bidding. Although they maintain that their God is very forgiving, they will be terrified by the possibility that he will punish them. This is the type of overwhelming fear that drives out reason and locks people into a closed loop of fear creating a belief which enhances fear. It will be good to be out of it at last.

# Chapter 9

# The Learning Paradigm

I have gone to great length to explain how we are driven by fear, but I would not want to give you the impression that this is the only driving force there is. Like the people who suggest the carrot and whip approach to motivation, I think that a model with two driving forces can be conceptually useful, but I would characterize them differently.

Let me use the example of a motorcar. There is a driving force that gets the car going and a controlling force that guides it and ensures that it goes where it should. In drawing an analogy between the car and society, I would make curiosity the driving force and fear the corrective force. We are driven by curiosity and controlled by fear. The interaction of these two forces is subtle, sometimes they reinforce each other and sometimes they oppose each other.

*Understanding Fear*

A baby crawling around a brand new world is fearless and driven by curiosity. As this baby learns, fear kicks in to protect it and guide learning along constructive paths. Sometimes fear overwhelms and stops the learning process, while the baby signals to its support services that help is needed.

But, as any systems engineer will tell you, control systems have their limitations and fear is no exception. Going back to the example of a car, if you are driving on a slippery road and you suddenly turn to the left, the car may go into a skid and continue on its straight line as dictated by its momentum and the loss of contact with its environment. The signals coming to you, the novice driver, indicate that the vehicle is not responding to your instructions and so you repeat the signal with greater emphasis. You turn the steering wheel more to the left. This then results in disaster because you have misinterpreted the signal. You should have understood, from the skid, that the car is unable to respond and this should have triggered a different corrective impulse. But fear kicked in and you panicked. Your subsequent reaction contributed to the problem.

*The Learning Paradigm*

After the crash you may refuse to get into a vehicle again, or refuse to try to drive one. While this would appear to be a ridiculous reaction to a car crash, it is a typical reaction in interpersonal relationships, or to learning mathematics, or grammar, or swimming. The trauma associated with a bad experience in one of these areas can change our approach to the subject for the rest of our lives and we seldom question or try to deal with it. Many people continue to close doors because of bad experiences throughout their lives. They gradually restrict themselves to a very boring existence. As they reduce their activities to rituals, they evolve strongly held, emotionally based opinions and refuse to listen to reason. All this severely restricts learning.

But the driving force can't be totally blocked. There always seems to be some curiosity left, even in the most extreme cases. Fear can block learning along certain paths, and can lock some people into a reclusive or aggressive closed loop, but it cannot achieve a total block on learning. This is especially true when we think of an entire community. Try to dam it and eventually the dam bursts. The major religions have all blocked learning, especially in the area of spirituality, for a very long time, but as the mushrooming list of publications on the subject attests, this dam is leaking. It won't be long before the old taboos are brushed aside and new ideas are readily accepted in this area. Other social restrictions are also being questioned, but we should not see this as the eve of destruction, rather it is a healthy sign that we are reexamining the traumas of the past.

By understanding the reasons behind the restrictions we will be able to change the rules with little chance of repeating past mistakes. We are learning more about our society and will soon get it under better control and pilot it into a new paradigm. Learning from our experiences in the war paradigm and carefully developing our spiritual concepts in parallel with whatever else is happening will build bridges into the future.

The maxim for the new paradigm is "maximize knowledge". To clear the way and make this process much easier, it will start with developing techniques for managing fear. This goal is already well established in our scientific community and can easily be widened to include non scientific methods and non-traditional areas of research and development. It is also likely that the pyramid shaped organizational structures that we have relied on to date will be replaced with a network structure, similar to that established with the Internet.

These changes will be accompanied by different approaches to social management which will result in a much more efficient social system. Resources, which are now tied up with the management and regulation of conflict and with delivering punishment, will gradually be released. These will be diverted to providing enhanced learning opportunities. It is also likely that there will be a closer integration between the traditional private sector organizations and learning institutions. This will result in both these organizations being very sensitive to the needs of the other.

With less emphasis on competition and more on cooperation, the productive sector will gradually evolve into larger and larger organizations, with much less formal structures. Instead of trying to maximize the return to shareholders, these organizations will try to maximize their own share prices.

*Understanding Fear*

This is more than a semantic change. By maximizing their share prices, the organizations will reduce their cost of share capital. This will require a very positive public image, which in turn will require much more information flow to the public. Control will be affected through customers exercising their choice. A choice based on factual data on the company rather than an impression formed by public relations specialists and delivered repeatedly through the media will influence the public's purchasing patterns.

While this is going on, major changes are taking place in the spiritual realm where I expect many advances will take place rapidly. It is these advances that will result in a quantum leap in the quality of life. Eventually the religious institutions will join the strategic alliance between the private sector and educational institutions and we will confidently embark on an unpredictable future. It is very exciting.

It is fun to try to predict what will happen in the spiritual realm. I expect that the idea of heaven and hell and a hierarchical structure of angels and saints with God at the top will be replaced with ideas more

*The Learning Paradigm*

reflective of the new structures that emerge in the community; perhaps similar to the Collective Unconscious suggested by Carl Jung. Our relationship with this Collective Unconscious will be structured in our imagination very similarly to our relationship with the information available through the Internet and our subconscious will be the communications link to it.

If these ideas are strange to you, try reading some of the references, such as "Exploring the Fourth Dimension" by John Ralphs; "The Power of the Subconscious Mind" by Dr. Joseph Murphy; or any of the books by Deepak Chopra, M.D. dealing with the way that the mind and the body interact such as "Quantum Healing". While this is all fascinating, it will depend on how quickly we can achieve control over fear and this won't be easy as it is such an integral part of our existence that we will be scared to investigate many of its realms.

For example, it will be necessary to understand what will happen to our economic activity if the new paradigm results in a reduction in greed. Would economic activity then diminish? If it did, would this lead to an economic depression, followed by enhanced fear? This is unlikely to happen. It is well established that increased confidence leads to enhanced economic activity. As the learning paradigm takes hold, it is very likely that economic activity will grow rapidly, especially in the area of education and research.

If we destroy the archetype of the Almighty God, what will happen with our super heroes, from Superman to Beckham? Will sports continue to play its present role in our lives or will the change in underlying philosophy lead to different forms of entertainment? I think that the era of the superhero will come to an end, but no one can really be certain.

The new paradigm will be characterized by individual self-determination. The icons of achievement that we have in our present society, college degree, fast car, beautiful woman, etc. will gradually lose their strength until they rank equally with the flow or activity goals. The tendency to express goals in terms of love, as in a *"All I want is someone to love"* type sentiment is indicative of this change; but I expect that the whole tone of the pop music love tragedy will reorient itself to deal with the learning to be derived from the social experience. Bob

Dillan's "Blowing in the Wind" and Bob Marley's "Emancipation Song" come to mind.

This self-determination will also be expressed in the fashion industry where it will be recognized that people will want a more personal communication to be signaled by their clothes; instead of having brand names prominently displayed, various icons or symbols will become popular as indicative of the interests and beliefs of the person wearing the clothes. This happens at present with rings, tiepins, broaches etc. being used to designate colleges and other tribal affiliations while T-shirts with various logos also help to communicate. The change I expect is that more personalized symbols will evolve so that the statement being made is not one of affiliation with an established brand image, but a more subtle, individual message. Perhaps there will be a combination of the two.

Every aspect of human behavior will be affected by these changes. Family life will evolve away from the concept that the man is the head of the household to one more akin with the structures described for the corporate world. The spiritual leadership now offered by the churches and other established religious bodies will either be lost, because they insist on being dinosaurs, or these organizations will evolve to once again become very involved with the spiritual development of individuals. There is certainly room for their participation and the resources that these institutions possess can easily be redirected to compliment the changes taking place in society rather than resisting them. It would be very interesting and rewarding to discuss spiritual matters with people who have spent their lives studying the subject, but this can only take place if they are willing to recognize the need to understand how fear affects people and how this has affected the church.

By far the hardest group to predict is the politicians. How will politics evolve in the learning paradigm? I have thought a lot about this and have come to the conclusion that politicians are very sensitive to the signals coming from the population and act in response to those signals. A politician recognizes that it is essential to be in power to have any effect on society and every effort is made to tell the population what they want to hear so that they will support the candidate with their vote. They are

*The Learning Paradigm*

skilled practicing psychologists and understand that they don't necessarily have to do what they promise. They simply have to demonstrate continuously that they are persuasive, confident, know where they want to go and are skilled at getting there. If the politicians sense that the people want to move into the learning paradigm, that is where they will take them. I expect that as these ideas get established in the community that politicians will quickly determine how best to use this new trend to maintain their power and will support the trend. Exactly how they will do this I am not sure.

# Chapter 10

# Strategy for the Learning Paradigm

The new paradigm will force all organizations to review their strategies. Each person will also have to review their own individual approach to life and decide how best to face the future.

The strategy outlined here is essentially an individual one, but it will have a strong influence on the strategies of corporations and other organizations. In this paradigm, each person has to develop their own individual goals. They cannot simply attach themselves to a pyramid and assume that the people above will provide nurture and direction. Instead, they have to do their own analysis based on their own unique point of view. Individual effort has to go into this process so that the result is a personal product. The prime goal is knowledge and this is pursued on several different fronts. Progress on each helps the other. They fall naturally into the following groups:

**Academic goals.** These challenge the intellect and develop it so that you can accept new ideas without being threatened by them. As you progress your self-confidence increases and after a while you question your teachers and take your own path, rather than following their direction.

**Physical challenges.** These include all forms of sports, exercise, hiking, camping etc. These provide other opportunities to test your skills and learn from others. The interface provides a forum for social interaction.

**Material wealth.** Some of us are so convinced that material wealth is the only goal that we focus on this to the detriment of other goals. The belief that we are winning urges us on. It is possible to follow this path for an entire lifetime, blind to any of the other alternatives available.

At the other extreme there are people believe that material wealth can only detract from personal growth and seek to have none. Many spiritual leaders have taken this path.

The norm is to want to ensure financial security for our dependents. It is the old survival instinct, but it is at the same time more than that. Because we think of making money as a challenge that rewards the winners, we look on material wealth as a status symbol. For a long time it was felt that it was God's will that produced wealth and rich people were considered to be particularly blessed. This has now changed and in some communities wealth is seen as evidence of an unsavory character as it carries the implication that this wealth was achieved through antisocial activity.

Wealth is useful. It can be used to support an extravagant lifestyle and sustain the illusion that we are "better" than the rest, or it can give the freedom to pursue personal interests. We will continue to seek wealth, but we will wish to use it more for personal development. As we become more sensitized to fear-driven behavior, we will naturally want to change what we do so that we don't reflect a high degree of fear. The fear of being seen as responding to fear will drive this change at a rapid pace.

**Personal growth.** This deals with emotions, feelings and confidence. As you experience life, you will need to reflect on your emotional reaction to the social environment; each reaction reveals something about yourself. By analyzing these responses, and applying the ideas on fear outlined earlier, you gain insights which help you to identify the social challenges which need to be overcome. These form the basis of a strategy for your own personal development. This has been the neglected area.

In all areas, targets are set and achievements recorded. Every success adds to our self-confidence. This must be built on personal achievements and not wholly on praise from others.

We need to feel good about ourselves, but it is very risky to base our self-opinions on the comments we get from others. We need these comments in order to shape our own self-opinion, but we must not fall into the trap of taking them at face value. We have to question what we are told about ourselves, analyze it, and study our own reactions to the information. This knowledge can be used to develop our own self-image and our self-confidence can be based on that. If we take the short cut of believing what we are told without the intermediate steps it is likely that we will be so dependent on the comments of others for our self esteem that we will be constantly seeking their approval. This will take us right back to the hierarchical structure and the war paradigm.

**Spiritual growth.** This is now a wide-open field. With the religious myths fading fast, new ideas are being generated at a rapid rate. The changing environment is inducing this and the trend will continue. This is a very important area and must not be left out.

It would be easy to point to all the damage that has been done by the religious myths. We may wish to stay away from this very dangerous area of the human experience, but this would eliminate a very powerful force for social evolution. Take for example the effect of the automobile. We could argue that this one item has caused more damage to human life than any other tool developed by man and that we should eliminate it. This could easily be supported by accident statistics. But it has also been a very useful tool and no one wants to be without it.

The same argument can be extended to other tools and just as we reject the arguments for the elimination of these tools, we have to reject the argument for the elimination of spirituality. It is indeed a very powerful tool and needs to be handled with care, but at the same time it is very useful and we need to gain a better understanding so that we can use it with greater skill.

If we follow the path of our ancestors we will adapt our spiritual beliefs to suite our social environment. At the same time we must be conscious of the effects that our spiritual ideas have on our society and expect that the marriage of the two may produce something totally unexpected.

The fascinating thing about this process is that each person can proceed on their own, without being a member of any particular group to facilitate the process. The attitude to life and other people which comes out of this approach is consistent with the behavior recommended in many religious texts. The rationale behind it allows us to drop the various conflicting ideas about spiritual beings that have been driven by fear and resulted in much war. Instead we can confidently be exactly what we are, without being driven by guilt or by some remote set of rules and rituals.

*These changes are enough to alter the whole pattern of society*

It is the age of individualism, not as a reaction to socialism, but as a new initiative, driven by a self-confidence which is based on rigorous analysis and experience and carefully crafted using all the skills developed by our civilization over thousands of years and preserved in rituals and folklore.

We live in a scientific era in which the concentration on logic and rationality has produced wonderful achievements, but these do not seem to be able to address our need for a purpose in life. The mechanistic approach of science, which seems to assume that the universe is running down like an unwinding spring, does not have much to offer in

*Strategy for the Learning Paradigm*

this area. This is where we have to rely on an alternative approach. We need to know that we have a purpose; that our efforts are not futile and that our skills are being applied to some cosmic design.

Science does not provide this. Nor does the ancient ideas advanced by religion hold sway any longer. A new path has to be sought which is consistent with the learning paradigm. We have to reconstruct a spiritual world that mirrors our current understanding of our physical environment and create a support mechanism that will help us face the future with confidence. This may not be essential if we are content simply to exist, but it will help us to face the stress of an uncertain future with greater confidence.

We can exit the war paradigm, but this path is not easy and very high levels of fear and uncertainty will have to be managed if we are to reject the ancient ideas which lead to the feelings of failure and self blame inherited with our beliefs. All the skills available to us will have to be consciously used to start the process that can result in our emerging from the mental prison of self-doubt into a new paradigm.

*Understanding Fear*

You must take the initiative, you must accept the consequences, you must decide if you want this challenge, you must decide when and how to start on this journey, how fast you will go, what direction you will take. You must understand that you are not trying to get to a specific target; there is no treasure at the end of the path. Instead you have the more difficult task of enjoying the journey, content that you will be travelling for as long as you remain a sentient being, and if we are to believe the stories coming from various sources, this journey may extend beyond physical death.

Because this path is unusual for our society, it will be difficult to find others to join you. This book is my attempt to make contact with other explorers.

I hope that I have convinced you that fear is a fascinating subject and worthy of study. You need to manage your level of fear, too little is as much a problem as too much. Raising the level of fear is relatively easy, but when it gets very high it is extremely difficult to control. Even as you experience the fear and understand what is happening, you may lose control, but this is inevitable, and becomes part of the learning experience that is all a part of the journey.

This path to self-development is a theme that is repeated in many different ways from diverse cultural sources. Each culture has their unique approach, but all seem to tackle the same problems.

A theme that is often repeated in religion is forgiveness. Christians understand that, to be good, they have to "forgive those that trespass against them", but very few achieve this because the method of achieving forgiveness is not explained. The literature seems to imply that the ability to forgive your enemies has to be achieved by direct force of will, or with the help of God. You have to constantly reject thoughts of revenge or "justice" as some people put it.

I suggest a different path. Instead of forcing yourself to be good, try to understand your environment and the fears that drive people to do the things that upset you. If you can appreciate that they are being driven by fear, it becomes almost natural for you to understand them and blame no longer exists. You will have in effect forgiven them by not attaching blame to their actions.

## Understanding Fear

After you understand how human behavior is affected by fear you have a much easier path to forgiveness, as when you understand what has driven a person to act violently the violent action is less of a threat. This understanding also gives you a path to take action, a path to deal with the threat.

Don Juan (Carlos Castaneda's character) has a different approach in that he seeks to disentangle the linkages between people by achieving complete self-confidence and self-reliance. This requires that you neither love nor hate the people you associate with, but are prepared to take full responsibility for yourself and not become upset if no one comes to your aid at a time of need. You also feel no obligation to help anyone although this does not mean that you will not help; just that you do not feel obliged to do it – you help if you want to help. A similar theme is present in the Celestine Prophecies where help is freely given with no thought of direct recompense.

Another theme of the people who have chosen to speak about the path of self-development is the rejection of worldly wealth. Mystics from many cultures have indicated that one of the signs of progress along the spiritual development path is the rejection of wealth. This is just as difficult to accept as forgiveness because accumulation of wealth is an integral part of our culture. We have seen the strife and hardship that poor people have to suffer and we don't want to find ourselves in that position. However, as we understand ourselves better and have a greater appreciation of how we fit into the environment, we will find that we can freely give a lot more than we presently do; as we get older and focus more on the spiritual path, this act of giving will become easier.

The act of giving is very emotionally rewarding, especially when the person receiving the gift appreciates it, but this is also very difficult to achieve. We all would like to give something that is appreciated, but we don't want to be gullible to con artists who play on people's instinct to help others. If you are remote from the person receiving the gift, the degree of satisfaction is much lower and in many cases you cannot be sure that your gift is satisfying some real need rather than create an additional dependence. All these act to reduce giving in a war paradigm. Contrast this with the giving that can take place in a learning environment.

*Understanding Fear*

In the learning paradigm knowledge is very valuable. This value does not disappear from the source when it is given away. It is easily multiplied with no detriment to the source, just like a piece of software. (Perhaps this is the symbolism that was aimed at in the story of the Sermon on the Mount.) Many learners can use (feed on) the knowledge without diminishing it. In fact it helps the growth of knowledge. The opportunity for someone to trick the giver is no longer relevant. This along with the low cost of information transfer makes giving, in the knowledge paradigm, much easier and less costly than in the war paradigm thus facilitating a process which is very rewarding for everyone involved. Perhaps it is this reward that encourages school teachers to work for relatively low pay. Perhaps it is this giving that takes place via the Internet that is the biggest influence for change in the Arab world today.

This theme of personal self-development is sometimes hidden or overshadowed by other features of a mystical or spiritual teaching. These other features are sometimes emphasized to achieve the acceptance of the ideas being advanced. In

Christian literature, the gospel according to Thomas, which is a secret gospel, illustrates a path to personal development, while the other New Testament gospels, the ones emphasized by the Church, seem to take a different path. They become increasingly political and hostile to Jews as they evolve from Mark to Matthew to Luke to John, a span of over 60 years. One of the things this illustrates is how the Christians fear of the Jews grew as their success threatened the Jewish community. It would appear that, as the strength of the Christians increased they became increasingly hostile and less forgiving.

Instead of the revolutionary philosophy of pacifism preached earlier in the Christian movement, these gospels illustrate the growing fear as the early leaders of the Christians faced increasingly hostile environments and responded with aggression. This fear induced some deviation from the mystical path of the teachings of Jesus. It must be an embarrassment to the church to have been forced, to its detriment, to form a link between the militaristic Old Testament and the pacifist New Testaments when it is very clear that New Testament doctrine has a totally different underlying philosophy to that of the Old Testament. This link was made to legitimize the new teachings and show that they evolved out God's accepted lineage. This was probably done in response to the criticism that the Christian upstarts had to face during the initial years. It is typical of new upstarts to try to illustrate connections to earlier ideas. It lends legitimacy and manages some of the fears.

The same theme of self-development is echoed in the teachings of Don Juan. Again a mystical or spiritual path of self-determination is described as Don Juan tries to get his student to follow his own individual path and to conquer fear. In some ways this path is better explained than in the New Testament.

If you intend to follow the path to knowledge you should be aware of the warning given by Don Juan, as recorded by Carlos Castaneda in "The Teachings of Don Juan - A Yaqui way of Knowledge". He illustrates that fear is the first opponent that has to be conquered, but goes on to explain that once fear is conquered there are other just as dangerous foes that have to be dealt with.

This emphasis on personal self-development is consistent with the learning paradigm and we could easily describe this whole philosophy as:

*A learning individual, in a learning organization, in a learning community*

All of the mystical paths to knowledge have techniques that can be used to manage the level of fear and it is a prerequisite that fear be controlled before progress can be made. Practice is essential for them to work effectively. Some ideas are discussed below.

One way to manage fear is to get angry. This may seem contrary to the whole intent of managing fear, but it really is not. Anger is a very useful mechanism and can work for you in many situations. It does not have to result from a loss of control as you can work yourself up into a controlled anger that drowns out fear and allows you to focus your intent clearly on a specific issue. Caution is thrown to the wind and you become very bold and some-

*Understanding Fear*

times self-righteous, but you can manage this. Politicians and lawyers often use this technique when trying to make an impressive speech as anger communicates well. We are all very sensitive to it. In this way anger can be used effectively to manage fear.

You should try this with caution as it can have a big effect on your personality. When you are angry you have great difficulty focusing on anything other than what has generated the anger. This makes you single-minded and directed, but it can also make you short-tempered and abrasive. This can easily result in you saying or doing something that you will regret later. More importantly it is quite possible to have your personality changed by habitual use of this skill once developed as it is very powerful and can create an addiction, just as some drugs can create an addiction. If you initiate this process in a discussion with a friend or spouse I advise not to break it off until the anger is spent and other emotions take hold. Take the whole rollercoaster ride – getting off in the middle can be disastrous.

The theme of overpowering fear comes through vividly in the novel "Dune" written by Frank Herbert. The book is about a desert planet and the various warring houses that get involved in a power struggle over its riches. In it he cites the following litany against fear.

> *"I must not fear. Fear is the mind killer. Fear is the little death that brings total obliteration. I will face my fear. I will permit it to pass over me and through me. And when it has gone past I will turn the inner eye to see its path. Where the fear has gone there will be nothing. Only I will remain."*

This litany is used when you feel that fear is taking control of you. It is intended to help you reduce fear to a manageable level, but it also illustrates the need to examine the fear or "turn the inner eye to see its path". It is this examination that results in our learning about ourselves and achieving personal growth.

You can develop your own litany to help you deal with the fears that bother you. Don't think that

*Understanding Fear*

you have to follow the guidelines of some expert or some ancient text; you are probably more highly trained than most of the people that wrote the ancient texts. In any case experts are only file servers, use them for reference not leadership. Self-determination is essential.

As you analyze the fear that controls you, it may occur to you that these fears are all associated with the things that you are fondly attached to like life, loved ones, riches, good health, your home, your country. Each thing that we are attached to makes us vulnerable as we are threatened when anything appears to harm any of these attachments. Each loved person or thing creates a chink in our armour, a hole in our shield through which our energy is lost. Don Juan recommends that we solve this problem by discarding all these loved items. When I was very young I owned a blanket to which I was very emotionally attached. Because of this attachment I was very frightened and vulnerable when this item could not be found. After I grew out of that dependence I was no longer vulnerable. It is a similar process that I think is being illustrated by Don Juan.

*Strategy for the Learning Paradigm*

The idea of isolating yourself from all the things you love, so that you would not be vulnerable to their loss, may at first appear revolting, but examine it carefully. If you have read Ann Rand's Fountainhead, you will have been introduced to a character who seems to live this ideal, as does Don Juan. It is an interesting concept and worth your further research.

❖ When trying to manage fear, it is important to realize that bravery is not the opposite of fear, it is simply a reaction to it; being brave indicates that fear is being managed and that you are still in rational control of the situation. It may be that you are in fact very frightened but can still act rationally, or, it may be that your natural reaction to fear creates a tunnel vision that reveals only one possible path out of the situation and that this results in brave actions. The combination of fear and action that relieves the fear leads to a feeling of well-being. We feel the flow of moving in the right direction.

*Understanding Fear*

> ❖ Many religious rituals use this process. They get everyone frightened (the devil is after you, you are a sinner, you will roast in hell, etc.) and then illustrate the one true path to salvation and encourage everyone to take it. The adrenaline released when everyone is frightened, followed by the action of singing, dancing, clapping hands, or chanting along with the repeated assurance that Jesus is looking after you is an excellent fear control technique as the aftermath of fear and action is usually an emotional high and everyone feels good after the ritual.

The power of belief, or faith, is very real. There are many instances in recorded history where faith has produced extreme effort and great reward. An essential component seems to be a belief that whatever the outcome you are a winner. If you die fighting for your lord, you will be rewarded in heaven. If you don't die you will be rewarded by physical pleasures and riches. This has the effect of removing the natural restraints induced by fear and allows unrestricted access to all our human resources.

Each culture has its own way to handle fear and I would postulate that the most successful cultures are those that are best at cranking up fear and then managing it. The English are good at individual fear management, as are the Americans, while the Japanese have discovered the skills necessary to work closely together as a group to manage their fear. Each technique is different and each has a powerful impact on society. Each culture has evolved its own way of dealing with fear. These vary from religious rituals, to pagan carnivals to the communal screams that come from the tabloid press.

If you "walk the walk", or in other words act out the role of a brave or confident person, you will help induce these feelings in yourself. Acting brave can help you to be brave, because it gives you another perspective, you can see the situation from a different angle, a new viewpoint. By acting brave, we can see how a brave person would access the situation and how they would act. This is made very easy if you have faith. An actor trying to perform a role in a drama tries to be that person, to understand how they feel, to believe what they believe, and to be frightened of what they are frightened of. Similarly, we can act out our beliefs through the use of faith.

I am fascinated by this thing we call faith. It is the best fear management technique I have come across and if you can get it working, you can expect a powerful effect. Because of the dangers associated with inventing an Almighty God, which are amply illustrated by the history of the church, I believe that it is better to have faith in yourself. But whereas the techniques for developing faith in a God are well developed, the means of developing self-confidence or faith in yourself are not. Any attempt to do this will therefore be an experiment, something that could go wrong, but if you manage your level of fear this will not be dangerous. In any event, all you do adds to your self-knowledge.

With increasing knowledge clearly defined as the goal, we need to experiment with belief systems which help to manage fear. If we follow the fractal pattern created by the changes in our own organizational structures that are currently underway, we can see the potential to produce radical changes in our society.

*Strategy for the Learning Paradigm*

We need to replace God/Devil, Heaven/Hell with the collective unconscious. This collective unconscious works and responds to your will. In some respects it behaves like the Internet with you as a powerful PC linked to one of the nodes. If you develop the skills you can browse this net; perhaps your dreams are produced by this type of activity. Just like the Internet you can find a lot of junk and what you browse may not be of any interest to you, but if you develop the necessary skill you will be able to make contacts which are useful.

Edgar Casey is the best recorded psychic browser that I have come across. He was able to get information that was used to help people with their medical problems. He would go into a trance and diagnose medical problems of people who visited him or wrote him letters and he would prescribe medicine, exercise, massage etc. to solve the problems. His prescriptions were remarkably successful, although there is confusion as to the exact process used to achieve the recoveries that took place.

Deepak Chopra ("Quantum Healing") and many other writers have written about the miraculous healings that occur in association with a positive change in mental attitude. Hope and confidence are powerful drugs. These may account for the success enjoyed by Edgar Casey, or it may have been some connection between him and the patient through the psychic net. ESP and astral travel also support the concept of a psynet which includes sites which are not a part of our physical existence.

> ❖ Although there are many recorded incidents of prayer of some form working to effect miraculous cures, access to this net is most apparent at the extreme ends of the fear-faith spectrum. A life of isolation, poverty and contemplation, which was the path of many mystics, can produce either extreme fear – the *"repent, the end of the world is at hand" group,* or it can produce extreme self confidence and a feeling of being a part of nature – the *Eastern mystic image.* Extremes in either direction seem to have been able to tap into the psynet and benefit from it, perhaps because of the strength of will and concentration that they achieve. When extreme fear is involved, energy seems to flow from the psynet to assist the person seeking it.

*Strategy for the Learning Paradigm*

❖ This is not something to worship, there is no suggestion here that the power and information available through the psynet is dispersed by a high ranking God. Instead I am suggesting it is freely available for those who seek it, but we need to understand more about the net and how to tap into it before we can really make full use of this source of information and energy. We appear to be able to send signals along the psynet which indicate what we would like to happen and these signals help to make our requests come true. It is the same idea as prayer. Both seem to depend on our absolute conviction that what we want is right for us. The force of faith shows up.

❖ As it did with the God figures of the war paradigm, the fractal pattern that flows from this structure will work its way into our daily lives and instead of setting up hierarchical organizations we will move more and more to networks. It is already happening in business. The private sector is a network of independent businesses under no single control, with no overriding hierarchical structure linking the companies together. It already has the network structure linking different companies together while it retains the hierarchical structure internally within the companies. It is this internal hierarchy that is now under investigation with much pressure being applied to adopt network or team structures.

❖ In this structure, experts in all fields lose their God-like status, but retain their function as an information source, conceptually similar to that of a file server in a computer network. This change also takes place in the spiritual world and the psynet is pressed into service. This reorientation cannot take place in a war paradigm as the absence of a leader will cause confusion, but as we manage fear this structure will become more and more acceptable

❖ This organizational structure is also supported by economic theory that illustrates that when rational, rather than emotional, economic decisions are made everyone is better off. The present economic environment approximates this closely, but in many cases fear blocks this process. The network organizational structure, combined with the other changes that fall naturally out of a learning paradigm, will result in totally different approaches to these aspects of human endeavor as well; I expect that there will be less effort placed on making laws and more on achieving cooperation.


❖ You will have noticed that I am using the same organizational pattern in the spiritual world as I expect will occur in the physical world. In doing this I have copied the process used by the ancients when they invented heaven and hell.

Just as the idea of the War God Yahweh was supported with a mythology, a similar process needs to take place with the new ideas. The psynet is part of this as is the concept of learning as our prime goal. Other similar concepts will be developed as the patterns emerge.

We have evolved our ideas of the spiritual by observing our environment and speculating on the nature of the entity that created it. In doing this we have assumed that the creator was an entity which we call God, but now that we know a lot more about nature we can evolve our ideas to accommodate this new knowledge.

To establish faith we have to achieve a certainty or absolute confidence. As we understand the patterns of life around us we develop this confidence and begin to have faith. Eventually we will believe with all our heart that we are on the right path when we are learning. This is the path dictated by our understanding of our environment and our unique ability to reason. We are in effect worshipping the reasoning process and celebrating its products rather than trying to interpret the wisdom of the elders. Faith in reason replaces faith in God, a process replaces an icon, but it is not a complete replacement and what results is a blend of the two.

This requires a lot of work. If you adopt a theory or belief without putting in the work it does not become a part of you and you never really trust it. Only after much toil, conversation, experience and speculation does it become ingrained in your psyche. I have met many people who have established confidence in beliefs that they have not thought through properly. When challenged to support their beliefs with logic they get frightened and see themselves as being surrounded by devils. Forced into a corner they become closed-minded and spend most of their intellectual efforts defending their beliefs. As people go through this process, sooner or later they become convinced that their opinion is a gospel truth and they don't want to change it. Unfortunately this leads to separation.

❖ This is recognized by Don Juan who warns against the blindness that follows success in the battle with fear; be warned and be cautious, but also be confident. It is helpful to think that your search for knowledge will continue after death, in another realm. This idea is a powerful tool, make full use of it. As long as you don't hand over your rationality to some higher authority you will be safe.

Do not leave with the impression that fear is something to be avoided. You must not run from it. Like a bullfighter, you must learn to master it through indirect attack. Fear is a dangerous weapon, but it is also a useful tool. We go to the theme parks to be frightened, because we enjoy the thrill. It is the same thrill we get from war, boxing, competitive sports, crime, driving fast, etc.; we need to be able to use it, but control it.

In your encounters with fear it is useful to be able to reduce your perception of the threats that constantly assail you from all directions. You have surely met people who seem to find something to be scared about at every possible opportunity; they are constantly voicing their fear and begging for assurance. While, at the opposite extreme, others seem to derive joy from their every action; their fears are buried deeply below the surface and only appear when there is great distress. These people don't have any fewer fears, they simply assess them differently and this allows them to get on with their lives in a happy, positive frame of mind.

After you assess where you are on the scale between these two extremes, you need to decide if you want to change. Should you decide to change yourself, first establish your goals as precisely as you can, then look for a book that gives you ideas on how to achieve your goals.

There are many of books on the subject, but I have always found them lacking in the process of establishing goals and this is why I advise setting your goals before you get into these books. They mainly prescribe action therapy and show you how to get active to achieve your set goals.

Action is a very good fear controller. Action works even if it is only physical exercise, but it is much more effective if it is directed at particular goals where there is a way of measuring progress so that you can evaluate how well you are doing.

# Bibliography

## *Business*

**Management and Machiavelli**, Anthony Jay, Century Business

**No Contest** The Case Against Competition: Why we lose in our race to win, Alfie Kehon, Houghton Infflin Company

**The Death of Competition**: Leadership and strategy in age of business ecosystems, James F. Moore, Harper Business

## *Religion & Spiritual*

**A History of God,** Karen Armstrong, Mandarin

*Understanding Fear*

**The Gospel According to Woman,** Karen Armstrong, Fount

**The Origin of Satan,** Elaine Pageles, Vintage Books, Random House Inc

**The Bible as History,** Werner Keller, Bantam Books

**The Messianic Legacy,** Michael Baigent, Richard Leigh & Henry Lincoln Corgi Books

**The Dead Sea Scrolls in English,** Geza Vermes, Penguin Books

**Reflections on Life After Life,** Raymond A. Moody, Jr. M.D., Bantam Books

## *New Age and Other*

**The Journey to the East,** Hermann Hesse

**Science and the Paranormal,** George O. Abell and Barrry Singer, Charles Scribner's Sons

*Bibliography*

**Quantum Healing,** Deepak Chopra, M.D., Bantam Books

**Is the Human Species Special? Why human-induced global warming could be in the interests of life,** Neil Paul Cummins, Cranmore Publications

**The Celestine Prophecy,** James Redfield, Warner Books

**Sophie's World,** Jostein Gaarder, Phoenix

**The Inner Reaches of Outer Space,** Joseph Campbell, Harper & Row

**Edgar Cayce: The Sleeping Prophet,** Jess Stearn, Bantam Books

**The Teachings of Don Juan,** Carlos Castaneda, Penguin

**The Middle Pillar** Israel Regardie, Llewellyn Publications

**The Communist Manifesto** Marx and Engels, Penguin Books

**Word Play,** Peter Farb, Bantam

*Understanding Fear*

**Enthusiasm Makes the Difference,** Norman Vincent Peale, Fawcett Books

**The Left Hand of Creation,** John D. Barrow and Joseph Silk, Penguin Books

**My Voice Will Go With You,** *The Teaching and Tales of H. Erickson* Edited with commentary by Sidney Rosen, W.W. Norton & Co.

**The Ascent of Man,** J. Bronowski, Macdonald Futura Publishers

**How To Stop Worrying and Start Living,** Dale Carnegie, Cedar

**Discovering The Future:** The Business of Paradigms, Joel Arthur Barker, I.L.I Press

**Finite and Infinite Games:** A vision of life as Play and Possibility, James P. Carse

**The Prince**, Nicclol Machiavelli, Penguin Books

**Exploring the Fourth Dimension:** Secrets of the Paranormal, John Ralphs, Llewellyn Publications

*Bibliography*

**The Power of your Subconcious Mind,** Dr. Joseph Murphy, Prentice-Hall Inc.

**What Happened in History,** Gordon Childe, Penguin Books

**Stress Without Distress,** Hans Selye, Signet

**Total Self Confidence,** Dr. Robert Anthony, Berkley

**A History of Sciences,** Stephen F. Mason, Collier Books

**Fractals, Chaos, Power Laws**, Manfred Schroeder, W.H. Freeman and Company

**The Decent of Woman,** Elaine Morgan, Corgi

**Supernature:** *A natural history of the supernatural,* Lyall Watson, Sceptre

**Supernature II,** Lyall Watson, Sceptre

**On Human Nature,** Edward O. Wilson, Bantam

**A Critique of the Idea of Progress: Ethics, Knowledge & Evolution,** Robert Nicholls, 123 Books

# About the Author

Dick Stoute holds a BSc from Concordia University, Montreal, an MBA from the University of Western Ontario, Canada, an MA from the University of the West Indies, Cave Hill Barbados, and is currently pursuing a PhD in philosophy at the University of Reading, U.K.

Dick has had a successful career in engineering and business. He retired early and is engaged in popularizing an insight that has had a profound effect on his own life. Violence is the product of fear. Someone who understands this will not want to demonstrate their own fear by being violent and will find ways to achieve their goals without being violent. This will lead to better family, community and business relationships. As society understands fear better, it will understand that the various forms of violent behaviour are all demonstrations of the perpetrator's own fear; this understanding will lead to support for violence being replaced by support for understanding.

Fear is to be understood, not fought. We need the right amount of it to make life exciting, but not so much that it makes us violent.

**http://understandingfear-das.blogspot.com**

www.ingramcontent.com/pod-product-compliance
Ingram Content Group UK Ltd.
Pitfield, Milton Keynes, MK11 3LW, UK
UKHW021257180426
11947UKWH00015B/895